FROM BEAN TO BAR

A CHOCOLATE LOVER'S GUIDE TO BRITAIN

FROM BEAN TO BAR

A Chocolate Lover's Guide to Britain

ANDREW BAKER

Published by AA Media Limited in 2019.

Text © Andrew Baker 2019.
The right of Andrew Baker to be identified as author of this work has been
asserted by him in accordance with the Copyright, Designs and Patents Act 1988.

A CIP catalogue record for this book is available from the British Library.

ISBN: 978-0-7495-8183-1

Publisher: Phil Carroll
Editor: Donna Wood
Designer: Tracey Freestone
Repro: Ian Little
Art Director: James Tims

Printed and bound in Dubai by Oriental Press

A05611

theAA.com

For my mother and father

CONTENTS

PROLOGUE

Chocolate is a wonderfully powerful substance. Its flavours and aromas can connect us instantly to the most treasured moments of our youth. The way that it melts in the mouth, transforming from solid to liquid at the temperature of the human body, is sensually satisfying in a way that no other food can match. And its near-mystical ability to comfort is a source of solace to millions.

It is no secret that the British love chocolate. We make 660 million kilogrammes a year here, and eat around 7.5kg each on average every year, putting us in the global top five of consumers. Much of what is made and devoured here is mass-produced rubbish: fat and sugar with a miserly cocoa content. But Britain is also a nation that makes – and eats – some of the very best chocolate in the world.

There is a quiet revolution going on among food producers in Britain, and craft chocolate makers are leading the way. This book aims to introduce readers to the people involved – and to tell you where and how you can discover the amazing and delicious chocolate creations that are coming to life all around us.

I want to take you on a tour of the kitchens, sheds and factories that are making chocolate from scratch – from bean to bar, as the process is known – using raw materials that are sourced with care, and with respect for the people who have grown them and for the land on which they have flourished.

Along the way we will take in some of the history of chocolate making in this country – which is where chocolate bars were first mass-produced – and some of the lovely things (not just bars, but filled chocolates, and bonbons, and brownies, and mugs of hot cocoa) that can be made with that wonderful substance.

The book is also a travel guide of sorts, because in travelling the length and breadth of Britain to meet artisan chocolate makers, I have found that they tend to practise their trade in beautiful and interesting places. It is not just what they make that rewards them, but how and where they make it.

My selection of chocolate makers is personal, and though it is based on years of delicious exploration, I know that I will not have included everybody's favourite. I hope, though, that anyone who has even a passing interest in proper chocolate – and good food in general – will find much here that is worth pursuing.

While I was working out my itinerary at the dining table at home, strewn with maps and opened bars of chocolate, my daughter Emily was at work in the kitchen, baking some of the excellent chocolate brownies with which she regularly blesses the household.

Every now and then I would break off from my map work to savour another square of dark, delicious chocolate and murmur compliments under my breath about balance, texture and melt rate.

"Dad," Emily eventually declared from the kitchen. "You are just a colossal nerd."

That's true, I had to admit, snapping off another chunk.

"But," she conceded, "you're a chocolate nerd, and that's no bad thing."

Welcome to my world.

BIRMINGHAM

IN SEARCH OF THE SWEET
TASTE OF CHILDHOOD

USEFUL INFO

Cadbury World
Linden Road
Bournville
Birmingham B30 1JR

cadburyworld.co.uk

By car: Parking on site

By train: 15-minute walk from Bournville Station, on the Cross-City Line from New Street

By bus: See travelinemidlands.co.uk

Open: Opening hours vary enormously and slightly weirdly, according to season, school term dates etc; check the website for details

The Chocolate Quarter
1A Spencer Street
Birmingham B18 6DD

thechocolatequarter.com

By train: A short walk from Jewellery Quarter Station, served by West Midlands Trains, Chiltern Railways and Midland Metro

Open: Opening days/hours somewhat limited: Wed–Sat, 11.30am–4pm

A WORLD OF WEIRDNESS

As I unwrapped the Cadbury Bournville bar I had great hopes that
I was revealing a time machine in chocolate form; a food that would
transport me, in the manner of Proust's lump of damp cake, back to
my childhood.

So much had changed since I last broke open the wrapper of a Bournville bar —
both for the chocolate, and for me.

The bar has shrunk as my waistline has expanded, and is now roughly the same
dimensions as a Yorkie or Milkybar. And the wrapper, once a sophisticated layer of
thick crimson paper around gold foil, is now utilitarian plastic.

So some of the magic has already gone, even before the bar itself is revealed.
Instead of pushing the gold-wrapped slab clear of its crimson sleeve and running
a thumbnail down the concealed furrow between the hidden chunks, I split the
plastic and fold back the crackling skin to reveal... Oh dear.

The bar within is dull brown, streaked with white, like an old wooden tabletop languishing at the back of a junk store. It is oxidised, meaning that it
has encountered changes in temperature as it slumbered on the shelf in the
confectioners' store at Victoria Station. This is not, of course, the fault of the
manufacturers, and does not render the bar unfit for consumption, which is just
as well, for eight months of its shelf-life remain...

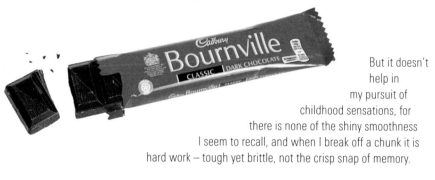

But it doesn't help in my pursuit of childhood sensations, for there is none of the shiny smoothness I seem to recall, and when I break off a chunk it is hard work – tough yet brittle, not the crisp snap of memory.

So I should not have been surprised that the flavour was also a colossal disappointment: bland and overwhelmingly sugary, a claggy mouthful of joyless excess. You can never go back.

I put the parody of Bournville aside. If I can't rediscover the bar of my youth, perhaps I can do justice to its name another way. By visiting, for the first time, Bournville itself, the village and factory built by the Cadburys to house and employ their army of workers in the heyday of Britain's most famous chocolate-making dynasty.

On the way up the M40 I stop off at Oxford services and buy another bar of Bournville. This has not suffered the same fate, and is at least the right colour. I snap off a chunk as I pull back onto the motorway, and try to recall why I ever found it attractive.

I think that the packaging had a lot to do with it. I was a pretentious child, and crimson and gold had adult connotations to my youthful brain. They were the colours on the smooth, flat, shiny packets of the Dunhill International cigarettes smoked by Elizabeth, my mother's most sophisticated friend. The surface of the desk in my father's study was dark red leather, tooled around the edges with gold filigree.

So the wrapper of a bar of Cadbury Bournville chocolate seemed to my seven-year-old self more alluring than boring Dairy Milk or supersweet Caramac. Similar ideas drove my experimentation with the Schweppes Bitter Lemon on the drinks tray.

I couldn't swear that I genuinely liked Bournville either to start with, but it soon became my chocolate of choice, and the smiley, comfortably proportioned lady in the junior school tuck shop knew that I (peculiarly, she thought) would look for a bar as my treat at Friday mid-morning break.

What was your childhood favourite sweet treat? Everyone has an answer to this question, and it almost always provides a shortcut to precious memories.

One day in the office, as an experiment that made me temporarily immensely popular, I laid out a mosaic of 'classic' chocolate bars and asked my colleagues to dive in, on condition that they told me which had been their choice as a youngster, what had appealed to them about it, and whether or not it still appealed.

> " What was your childhood favourite sweet treat? Everyone has an answer to this question

Not everyone had shared my British upbringing, and there were one or two complaints about the absence of Hershey's or Crackers or other exotica, but almost everyone found a bar that flicked a switch of reminiscence. You do not have to be a psychologist to understand that some of the most memorable sensations of childhood will be those associated with reward, with relaxation, or with rationed or rarely sanctioned sweetness.

I have found at numerous taste tests that if you want to get people talking about chocolate you offer them an artisan bar from an exotic maker or location. But if you want to get them talking about their childhood, or just help them to make friends, you offer them junk in iconic wrappers.

As you might expect, the initial response to my bonanza of bars in the office was enthusiastic ("Free chocolate!") but after the hubbub died down and as the first few mouthfuls were taken on board, mixed feelings emerged.

All I had requested the freeloaders to do was to nominate their childhood favourite, and taste it again with their senses alerted. All I asked was: "Do you still enjoy it?"

Given the fact that these were high-functioning adults, some of whose jobs involved the interpretation of sophisticated foodstuffs for discerning consumers, a surprising number said "Yes".

Perhaps that is just my chocolate snobbery coming to the fore. It is a source of near-constant amazement to me that, given the widespread availability of good chocolate, people still insist on filling their faces with bad chocolate – or at least indifferent chocolate that has been aggressively bulked out with fat, sugar and cheap inclusions.

It's none of my business, really, and just as I take pleasure in sharing obscure bars of artisan this and exotic-origin that with friends and workmates, it was great fun to see the childlike joy prompted by the pile of junk. I said that I could never go back, never recreate the pleasure that I derived from savouring a bar of Bournville in a Hertfordshire garden.

Watching a trio of hardened news reporters squabbling over a Milkybar, it was clear that some had never left.

For me, though, the magic had faded. My second bar of Bournville, consumed with due care and attention on the M40, was better than the first – it wasn't an oxidised brick, which helped – but it wasn't the bar of my childhood.

Finishing the last chunk, I followed the signs for Birmingham (South), and before long was on the fringes of the village that gave the bar its name.

Approaching Birmingham from this direction – and so avoiding the trauma of Spaghetti Junction – you will come across Bournville between the starkly urban semi-dereliction of Stirchley and the students-only enclave of Selly Oak. It is still entirely recognisable as the village planned by the Cadburys on what was then the outskirts of Birmingham more than 100 years ago.

This is a pilgrimage well worth making for chocolate fans of all ages, because it offers two treats of very different natures.

Bournville the urban village surrounds the Cadburys Bournville factory, which itself is host to Cadbury World, Britain's only chocolate-fixated theme park.

The village is a charmer, fascinating in many different ways. Cadbury World is a horror show, but in the right company an entertaining one.

Bournville is a model village – not a tiny community but 'model' in the sense that the Cadburys hoped it would serve as a model for other industrial communities.

John Cadbury opened a grocer's shop in Bull Street in Birmingham in 1824, when George IV was on the throne and chocolate was prepared with a pestle and mortar and consumed with hot water. Mr Cadbury, a Quaker, was particularly keen on hot chocolate because it was an alternative to alcohol, which his faith regarded as evil.

He was clearly good at making it, for the business flourished and he diversified into various forms of cocoa and drinking chocolate, moving production into a factory in Bridge Street – still in the centre of the city – and joining forces with his brother Benjamin.

The business thrived and eventually John handed control to his sons Richard and George. The latter, something of a business visionary, saw that they needed a new factory, and believed that it should be quite different from the 'squalid and depressing' surroundings of central Birmingham.

The Cadburys' cocoa arrived by train from London, and the milk they used was shipped on canal boats, so in the late 1870s they established their new works around Bournbrook Hall, four miles south of Birmingham and close to Stirchley Street railway station and the adjacent Worcester and Birmingham Canal.

The factory and its surrounding community grew together. George declared that a tenth of the vast site should be laid out as parks, recreation grounds and open spaces, and that the cottages in which his workers would live should have the appearance of a 'garden village'.

The Cadburys employed a resident architect, William Alexander Harvey, and by the turn of the century the estate, now occupying 330 acres of land, comprised more than 300 cottages and houses. Many more houses and ancillary buildings in the same red brick were built before World War I, with smaller, still sympathetic developments continuing through much of the 20th century.

This is the Bournville that the visitor sees today: a homogenous, attractive, functioning community, adjacent to but not overshadowed by the vast factory, and set among parks and recreation areas that are well kept and clearly in enjoyable and frequent use. The community is centred on a village green, faced by a row of slightly twee but healthily functioning shops and flanked by a splendid Quaker Meeting House – the equivalent of a parish church. Over the road from the green is a magnificent carillon of bells, shiny and in loud working order. There are no pubs, for George, like his father, was a staunch temperance Quaker. "Who needs liquor?" he might have demanded of his thirsty workers. "Here we have green fields, healthy sport and God's own hot chocolate."

It is a lovely village that George and his family built. And it should be said that the company, although these days owned by the faceless international food conglomerate Mondelez, still plays an important role in the community, not just in Bournville but in Birmingham as a whole.

After an enjoyable stroll around the village green and a look at Selly Manor, the 14th-century house transferred here by the Cadburys from nearby Bournbrook and now a nifty little museum, it was time to confront the looming presence for which, and around which, this community had been built: the Bournville factory itself, and Cadbury World, which it houses.

For this part of the trip I felt I needed moral support, and it was unsurprisingly easy to recruit my daughter Lucy, a graduate of the University of Birmingham now at work on an MSc in forensic psychology and an expert, like her sister Emily and my wife, on Cadbury products.

> " On the breeze there was the scent of sugar, and fat, and a hint of cocoa – the aroma, such as it is, of Cadbury chocolate

Cadbury World occupies a wing of the Bournville factory itself, and we parked next to the looming hulk of the great manufactory. It was an afternoon in September, grey and drizzling relentlessly. It was hard to see through the frosted glass of the factory windows whether anything was being manufactured within, but then Lucy told me to sniff the air… and on the breeze there was the scent of sugar, and fat, and a hint of cocoa – the aroma, such as it is, of Cadbury chocolate.

"It's sort of an urban myth that you can smell that in Selly Oak when the wind is in the right direction," Lucy said. "But I've lived here more than three years, and this is the first time I've ever caught it." It was oddly reassuring, if not exactly pleasant.

The entrance foyer was strangely deserted, but from across the hall, close to the exit, came the excited buzz of a massed school party descending on 'the World's Biggest Cadbury Shop' like a plague of blazered Brummie locusts.

We purchased our tickets and filed obediently through the zig-zagging queue system – although there was no queue to organise, we are British and it seemed the right thing to do – and through the swing doors into Cadbury World itself.

I am not sure what I was expecting – perhaps a cavernous industrial space, or a hall of Technicolor wonder like the movie version of *Charlie and the Chocolate Factory*, with Willy Wonka stepping forward to welcome me. I was not expecting to walk into a clumsily ersatz Amazonian rainforest.

But that is where we found ourselves, confronting a dummy Mayan holding a cacao pod to the sky, as if marvelling at the profits it would one day generate for a faceless multinational. Around the next corner the Aztecs were involved too, and 'Quetzalcoatl's Bridge' abutted a garden-centre pond.

It seems to be an unbreakable law of human behaviour that if you put a shallow body of water in a public space, people will lob coinage into it. I couldn't see any sign demanding a tribute to the gods of the Aztecs (or Mayans), or soliciting charitable donations, but the citizens of Birmingham evidently felt compelled to flip their spare change into the still waters here.

Above the shiny coins on the pond's still surface floated a cut-out Freddo the Frog, either a previously unheralded central American deity or a refugee from an attraction that still lay ahead.

For our journey had barely started. The conquistadors (vaguely Hispanic shop-window dummies) showed up to rip off the native Central Americans and infect them with ghastly European diseases, the cacao was loaded aboard wooden ships and in a trice we were in the London of Samuel Pepys, where the diarist and incorrigible roué was curing a hangover with hot chocolate.

In due course a youthful Cadbury World employee emerged from behind a screen and ushered us out of the fake London square, where two-dimensional aristocrats sipped at flat cups behind the plastic windows of 'White's Cocoa House', and into a kind of lecture theatre with bench seating arranged in a semicircle around a small cinema screen.

The lights dimmed and a spotlight illuminated a large lump of vaguely featured plaster protruding above the stage. The lump began to address us, rather in the manner of the ill-formed and barely manifested Voldemort struggling to reassert himself in the early Harry Potter films.

But this was not the Dark Lord. It was instead the cod-Victorian tones of George Cadbury himself, whose features eventually caught up with his pronouncements when the projector finally kicked in and played onto the rudimentary hologram base.

George took us through the history that I have recounted above, with polite interjections from actors playing his sons on screens to either side. It was jolly dull.

And so was the next presentation, in a next-door theatre, in which a cartoon scientist took us through the chocolate production process. The gimmick here was that the seats moved at suitably dramatic moments.

One can imagine that the work of many focus groups, ideas kickarounds and brainstorms is manifested in Cadbury World, but the overwhelming impression remains that of a slightly desperate repurposing exercise for redundant areas of a gigantic and outmoded factory.

Either that, or the minds behind the project started with the one sure-fire hit – an enormous emporium full of cheap chocolate – and then tried to come up with things to put in front of it. The whole shebang is an exercise in delayed gratification, so that visitors are taunted with chocolate throughout the process, with each new stage further delaying the climax: the exit through the gift shop.

Some of the attractions en route to this consummation are dreary in the extreme: the 'manufacturing' zone is just videos of zillions of buttons and bars emerging from machines; and the only machine that one actually meets is a 1950s mixing vat of admirable girth which these days, as Lucy sharply observed, stirs only a large disc of chocolate-coloured shiny plastic.

It is not the fault of the demonstrators that what they are demonstrating is mundane, but it is a shame that their raw materials are not only rubbish but inedible rubbish at that. The youths who took us through elementary tempering and squiggling skills had mastered their limited briefs – clearly aimed at their

usual audience of massed schoolchildren – but they were working with rather tired molten Dairy Milk, which minimised any aura of glamour.

And the sense of privilege was utterly banished by their rote pronouncements that the mixture was 'for demonstration purposes only' and not to be consumed. No dipping!

We were gifted a splodge of the mixture in a tiny paper cup 'with the addition of your choice' (I took biscuit crumbs, then took a mouthful, then threw it away) before an endearing young lady ran through an evidently well-practised routine with some old filled-chocolate moulds from the factory. Again, we didn't get to taste the results – gratification delayed once more.

We posed atop a surfboard in front of a green screen that would superimpose us on a wave of chocolate – an image so disturbing that I declined to fork out £10 for a permanent version – and then proceeded to the only element that truly resembled a full-on theme park – a sit-aboard ride called Cadabra.

This is where the creative types in the Cadbury marketing team had been given free rein – and perhaps some mind-altering drugs. The result was a slow-motion tour through the world of the Chuckle Beans, who were essentially oversized plastic Creme Eggs with rictus grins.

The Beans had been distributed around a seemingly random landscape with little discernible relation to either Cadbury or chocolate, and were joined in these locales by dippy co-stars: here a chorus line of dim-witted cows; there a sunglassed and perhaps stoned cockerel. Beans popped incomprehensibly out of windmill towers and swayed in dayglow suburban gardens; one had apparently had enough and was trying to end it all by plunging from a ski lift.

We motored through these bizarre and charmless scenes aboard a large-scale Toytown car, a sort of ChoccyNoddymobile. We had been admonished to keep our extremities out of danger but Lucy whooped throughout, shooting video and stills from her phone for immediate transmission to her social media audience.

"Camera! Smile!" she yelled, but she didn't mean her phone. A flash erupted from behind a Bean. Blast. Captured.

Dazed and confused, we were helped from our vehicle by another solicitous young Brummie (in the course of our stay, staff seemed to outnumber visitors by a ratio of approximately 20 to one), who directed us to a booth where we could purchase a print of the Cadabra snap for just £10. I offered twice that to destroy the negative, but the operative didn't know what a negative was.

It was almost over. Perhaps it was delayed shock from the onslaught of the Chuckle Beans, but I was strangely affected by Advertising Avenue, where we were bombarded with music and images from Cadbury campaigns of the ancient and not-so-ancient past: Terry Scott (remember him?) dressed as a schoolboy and waving a Curly Wurly (remember them?). Bow-tied Frank Muir extolling the virtues of the Fwuit & Nut bar. That lady with the suggestive Flake bar… and then the unmistakable strains of 'In The Air Tonight' sounded as we rounded a corner to see a fake gorilla slumped listlessly behind a drum kit.

Cadbury's musical primate clip from 2007 was voted the greatest ad of all time by the panel of the British public convened by *Marketing* magazine, and the brains behind the theme park would have done well to erect a plaque to that effect with the original production playing behind it.

Instead they had a dummy DJ cueing up discs to announce it, and then the poor hairy robot jerked into life and rather feebly attacked his kit at the appropriate moment. Say what you like about Phil Collins – and no doubt he is still enjoying the royalties – but he was much better with the sticks than an animatronic primate.

And so, via a few confusing moments in (or on) Purple Planet, an almost entirely pointless interactive zone, to the World's Biggest Cadbury Shop, a purple paradise for devotees of indifferent-quality chocolate, in which we were, once again, the only punters.

I loaded Lucy with a colossal bar of Dairy Milk as a reward for her company, and stocked up on Buttons for her sister and a hand-decorated but frankly not greatly impressive souvenir 'With Love' plank for my wife.

Once again, as on our way in, we progressed in a zig-zag down a long and utterly unpeopled queue-organising line to the till. The young man on duty seemed pleased to see us.

"Is it always this quiet?" I asked.

"It depends," he said. "This morning we had five school parties. That wasn't quiet at all." His eyes glazed over at the thought, and we headed for the car park.

On the way back to her student house in Selly Oak, Lucy asked if she might have the six slim bars we had been handed at various stages on our journey. "Freebies," she cooed, appreciatively.

I could hardly begrudge her them – and I certainly didn't want them myself – but it was strange how even I felt obscurely grateful to have exited the experience with half a dozen free bars of chocolate. After a total expenditure of £74.

I could hardly complain about that: all transactions had been willingly entered into, and even the souvenir photograph had a certain macabre charm. But I can't say that it felt like good value.

What I found more disturbing, though, was the notion that the vast majority of customers at Cadbury World that day had been not consenting adults but schoolchildren, who were there on organised (and presumably subsidised) 'educational' visits.

No doubt they had learned some useful history about their home city, and taken on board a sense of what capitalism with a benevolent face can bring to its workers. They had also been told some very basic facts about cocoa growth and chocolate production.

But nowhere had they learned who owned the factory they were walking around, or how it had been acquired, or where the profits that it generated went to. And at no time had it been pointed out that chocolate doesn't have to be adulterated with huge quantities of sugar and vegetable fat, and that it can taste better if it isn't.

And it certainly hadn't been mentioned that for all the wonders of the Bournville factory in the leafy model village of Bournville founded and nurtured by the Cadbury family, the bar of Bournville chocolate sold by Mondelez, owners of the name, brand and factory, is these days made in France.

Personally, I find it counterproductive to cultivate rage against faceless multinational conglomerates and their activities. They don't take any notice, and it does nothing for my mood.

Direct action is the best response – and I don't mean torching factories or dressing up as a Creme Egg to picket the confectionery aisle in Tesco. I mean seeking out proper chocolate – chocolate made by good people in the right way – and ideally sold in an actual shop staffed by actual humans and serving an actual community.

But in Birmingham, cradle to the most famous brand in British history, this is not easy to achieve. I had consulted the hive mind of chocolate aficionados on Twitter, and come up with just one recommendation for first-class chocolate in England's second city: Chocolate Quarter, to be found, I gathered, in Birmingham's Jewellery Quarter.

It is a nice little shop, run by very well-meaning people, and it makes perfectly acceptable chocolates of no great distinction. If you are in the neighbourhood I certainly recommend that you pop in (though do consult the rather limited opening hours first) and encourage the owners in their efforts. It is far better in almost every way that I can think of to spend money in Chocolate Quarter than in Cadbury World.

Yet it seems a shame (without any disrespect to Chocolate Quarter) that one little shop selling soft centres made with decent bought materials is the best that Birmingham, a city with some claim to being the cradle of industrial chocolate consumption, can do.

Thinking this over on the way out of the city (having left my daughter cackling over her freebies like a sugar-crazed Gollum), I wondered whether York, that other melting pot of chocolate history, might turn out to be more rewarding.

☐ You can evoke the flavour of a Cadbury's Old Jamaica bar with Chocolate Quarter's filled chocolate of the same name; if you are feeling brave you could sample their Bear Grylls cricket praline (it refers to the insect, not the game). Boxes of mixed truffles range from £6 to £37.50.

☐ Obviously I can't stop you buying Cadbury chocolate for personal consumption, but if you have to inflict it on others about the only responsible way to do so is to melt some Dairy Milk in a bowl over hot water, then dip chunks of fruit – strawberries, pineapple, mango – in the chocolate and twirl around until they set. Chill and serve.

TASTING NOTES

☐ Check out the opening times for Chocolate Quarter – they are limited. The bars are fairly unremarkable, but there are some interesting filled chocolates.

☐ Better yet, if in Birmingham, go to Hotel Chocolat at New Street Station or in the Bullring and buy two bars of supermilk from the Selector section. It's £3.95 for two, but then you won't need to spend any money on fruit to disguise the taste...

WHAT IS GOOD CHOCOLATE?

You may have gathered from my reaction to Cadbury World that I am not a big fan of mass-produced chocolate. Let me explain why not.

Pick up a bar of Dairy Milk or Galaxy (they won't be hard to find) and DON'T OPEN THE WRAPPER. This may be hard for you, but there is a purpose.

Look at the wrapper. Think about what it says – and what it doesn't say. One says 'Dairy Milk' in large letters, and the other says 'Galaxy' and then, in smaller letters, 'Smooth Milk'. Neither of them says 'Chocolate'.

Yet if you ask anyone what these objects are, they will say 'chocolate bars' or 'bars of chocolate' and look at you as if you are a bit loopy.

They are not really bars of chocolate, though. Turn over the Galaxy and look at the list of ingredients, which are identified, by law, in order of quantity contained.

The first ingredient in the Galaxy bar – the thing that it contains most of – is sugar. Turn over the Dairy Milk. The first ingredient is milk. Fair enough. Well done, Cadbury. The second ingredient is sugar.

So neither of these is really a chocolate bar, because cocoa-related components (cocoa butter and cocoa mass) are secondary ingredients. What you are buying when you buy one of these bars – and many other mass-produced bars like them – is a bar of sugar and fat. Yet we don't say to ourselves, "Oh, I could murder a sugar and fat bar."

Both of these products are made by vast multinational corporations: Mondelez (formerly Kraft) in the case of Dairy Milk, and Mars in the case of Galaxy. They are manufactured by gigantic machines in colossal factories from ingredients bought in bulk.

The people who 'make' the chocolate (or supervise the machines that do so) do not know where the beans they are using came from. What they are producing must conform to a bland flavour template that has little or nothing to do with the distinctive characteristics of the raw materials employed.

This is not good chocolate. You can put down the Dairy Milk or Galaxy now. I said… oh, never mind.

I don't enjoy eating this kind of chocolate. I'm not attacking those that do – it's a free world, and some of these products' most avid consumers are related to me – but I really, truly, don't like them.

When I eat a chunk of mass-produced 'milk' chocolate (under protest, and for research purposes only), I taste sugar and fat; I'm aware of the lurking presence of palm oil and soya lecithin, and often of other additives preceded by the letter E. The texture is gloopy and it sticks to the roof of my mouth. The aftertaste is cloying and weird.

The chocolate I like to eat contains more cacao-related stuff (beans and cocoa butter) than anything else. I like to know that the person who made it cared about what they were producing; that they knew something about where all their raw materials have come from; and that they treated those raw materials, and the people who grew them, with respect.

The shorthand phrase that I often use to describe my kind of chocolate is 'good stuff made by good people in the right way'.

It's not enough for the makers simply to be virtuous – I take my own pleasure seriously, and it is entirely possible for chocolate that is ethically A-OK to taste pretty ghastly, in which case we praise the attitude but encourage some attention to the methods.

And it's not enough for the makers to be expert – delicious chocolate leaves a nasty aftertaste if people or the environment have been damaged in the course of its growth and manufacture.

The good news is that chocolate that is made by good people in the right way is no longer hard to find. And the better news, if you live in the UK, is that you do not have to travel too far to find it.

Over the last decade or a little more, there has been a revolution in the chocolate world. Consumers have gradually become aware that not all chocolate has to taste the same, and that really good chocolate does not come from the vast, established manufacturing behemoths – or even from the famous names in posh chocolate from Belgium and Switzerland.

Really good chocolate comes mostly from small set-ups that employ a handful of people. These little organisations have direct links with the people who grow the cacao beans and the sugar that they use. They often encompass other ethical concerns such as respect for energy generation, and they certainly take care of the health and wellbeing of their employees.

The UK now has a good number of such organisations, and a far greater number of people who appreciate what they do and what they make, and work to spread the word. There are shops and cafes that sell great chocolate bars and gorgeous cups of hot chocolate, and bakeries that use only the best chocolate in their cakes. There are tasting clubs that taste fascinating bars from all over the world, and online suppliers who source deliciously obscure bars from tantalising new sources.

In short, this has become a great country in which to enjoy truly good chocolate. But we mustn't be complacent about that. Making artisanal chocolate is always a labour of love, and very rarely a route to riches. The people who choose this hard path do so because they enjoy what they do and what they make – but they need and deserve our support if they are to thrive – and in the process of thriving, to benefit thousands of people in cacao-growing countries who deserve a more prosperous and sustainable future in return for all their hard work.

So the next time you are about to purchase a bar of chocolate, think for a moment about what you are buying. Is it mostly sugar and fat? And is that really what you want? If it is, good luck. But if it isn't, and you would rather enjoy a bar that tastes distinctively delicious, that reflects the character of the land that produced it and which properly rewards all those who made it… read on.

YORK

ANCIENT AND MODERN

USEFUL INFO

York Cocoa Works
10 Castlegate, York YO1 9RN

yorkcocoahouse.co.uk

By car: 5 minutes' walk from St George's
Field car park, Fishergate, York YO10 4AB.
Blue Badge holders may park directly opposite
the Cocoa Works on Castlegate

By train: 10–15 minutes' walk from York mainline station

York's Chocolate Story
3–4 King's Square, York YO1 7LD

yorkschocolatestory.com

01904 527765

By car: 10 minutes' walk from St George's
Field car park, as above
By train: 10–15 minutes' walk from
York mainline station

Open: 10–5pm every day; check website for public
holiday opening times

Monk Bar Chocolatiers
7 Shambles, York YO1 7LZ

01904 634999

Open: Mon–Sat 10am–5pm; Sun 11am–4.30pm; closed Tue

Bullion
Cutlery Works, 73–101 Neepsend Lane, Sheffield S3 8AT

bullionchocolate.com

THE STORY CONTINUES

Of England's great chocolate cities, York is my favourite. It combines colossally significant heritage in the confectionery industry with an energetic, good-humoured and open community of present-day makers. All of this lines up with a compact, beautiful and civilised city centre to make a destination that should be right at the top of every chocolate tourist's list. I cannot think of anywhere better in the UK to make, buy and enjoy a bar of fine chocolate.

It helps that the city and its highlights – chocolate-related and otherwise – are tremendously accessible. However you arrive in York you will quickly find yourself right at the centre of the action, within the old city walls. There is so much for the chocolate lover to see and do, and it is a good idea to do a spot of research either before you come or as soon as you arrive.

There are leaflets at the train station, and signposts close to car parks, directing visitors to York's Chocolate Story, the visitor centre at the heart of the old city that celebrates the sweetest of local histories. On the way you can call in at contemporary chocolatiers who are continuing – and in some ways improving upon – the traditions of their forebears.

The history of chocolate in York is every bit as eminent, and in some ways more ancient, than that of the more celebrated Bournville in Birmingham.

This is the city of Rowntree's and Terry's, and other forgotten but once equally powerful brands – and the city of Mary Tuke, the remarkable woman who started the whole story off. It's significant, I think, that York's chocolate destiny was first shaped by a determined woman almost 300 years ago, because its future is being defined by strong women today. And as a visitor you can choose which way you wish the narrative to run: from today back to yesteryear, or starting deep in the past.

Perhaps, like me, you prefer to operate in a chronological manner. In that case, postponing the delights of chocolate present (and ignoring, if you can, the other delights of York's ancient past, which are many and varied), head first to York's Chocolate Story, which is housed in a modern building of no great character close to the top of the city's most celebrated olde worlde street, the Shambles.

Unlike Cadbury World, this is not a repurposed chunk of a functioning chocolate factory. But what it lacks in authenticity it more than makes up for in warmth of welcome, because all visits to York's Chocolate Story are guided not by signs and interactive machines, but by real, live, wisecracking Yorkshire folk.

You may, like me, find the prospect of human guidance somewhat awkward. I am English, and therefore regard the idea of interaction with people to whom I am not related with profound suspicion. But even though I was not concealed within a larger group – was accompanied, in fact, only by fellow visitors Geoff and Joan, local people of an even greater vintage than myself – the entire experience was thoroughly enjoyable, and barely embarrassing at all.

It helped, perhaps, that we were the last visitors of the day to be conducted around by our guide, a fellow by the name of Lee who was, he rapidly, accurately and disarmingly confessed, "built on the Brian Blessed scale".

Lee met us on the ground floor, adjacent to the gift shop, and ushered us into a lift. On the top floor we disembarked to find ourselves on a cobbled street, an indoor set constructed to mimic an urban thoroughfare of the early 20th century, facing two bowed shop windows crammed with the chocolate boxes and wrappers of yesteryear.

Among the items in the window was one that made me catch my breath – and instantly transported me in my mind's eye to the bedroom of a little old house in Hertfordshire early one Christmas morning, many years ago...

How many years ago? It's quite rude to ask, and you have broken into my golden-hued reminiscence. *Many* years ago. Black-and-white television. Dinky Toys. The Beatles, still together and pre-beards.

And, at the end of my little brother's bed and mine, promisingly lumpy bundles. Children of privilege that we were, on Christmas Eve Santa delivered not only filled stockings but also pillowcases stuffed with covetable goodies.

Sated with a lifetime's consumption, it is the stockings that I remember most clearly. They were actually my father's gigantic hiking socks, pale green and thickly knitted, and with an admirable capacity for treats.

It was a great thrill to feel around the solid lumps and bumps on the exterior and try and work out what was inside. One substantial cube was always there, about halfway down, revealed, after frenzied excavation of the upper layers, as the most exciting chocolate treat of my youth, and the most enduringly powerful memory of my childhood Christmases: a Terry's Chocolate Orange.

Part of the appeal was the complex wrapping: within the cardboard cube a sphere wrapped in proper metal foil, and within that (if it was unpeeled with sufficient patience and care) an intact, shiny brown sphere, dimpled (am I imagining this?) like the skin of a real orange.

It was important to me that it should be intact, because I vividly remember the satisfaction of sitting the whole orange in the centre of its foil, and giving the very top of the sphere a gentle flick with my index fingernail so that it fell, as if by magic, into segments.

These brother James and I would devour – not frantically, but with a certain level of reverence. Partly because they were the only sugary treats that our stockings contained, partly because they were more 'grown-up' in taste than our Milkybars and Dairy Milks, but mainly because, like Santa, this chocolate arrived just once a year, and every segment had to be savoured.

Lee, the Chocolate Story guide, had been trying to attract my attention. Suddenly I was no longer at the top of The Old Cottage at Hadley Highstone, but once again with my nose pressed to the glass of an ersatz shop window on the second floor of a modern building in York.

"I said, 'Have you noticed what's next to the chocolate orange?'" He directed my gaze. Another cardboard cube, another foiled sphere within. Terry's Chocolate... Apple?

"It came before the orange," Lee said. "1926 to 1954, they made the apples, then they finally realised that the orange worked a lot better."

The orange itself, sad to relate, is no longer made in York. I still buy them at Christmastime, though the taste is disappointing and the wrapping is bland. I picked one up in a supermarket the other day out of curiosity and examined the label, hoping to see that it still came from the city of its invention. But no. It's made by

Carambar & Co, whoever they are, in the rue Maurice Mallet in Issy-les-Moulineaux in France. Harrumph.

The orange is far from forgotten in York, though. It lives on in the museum, and in the inhabitants' fond memories – and on the site of the old Terry's factory on the outskirts of the city, now replaced by smart upmarket flats, where the water feature in the courtyard takes the form of a giant chocolate orange in bronze, with a fountain playing on a fallen segment.

Lee wanted to know what our favourite chocolates were – Christmas treats didn't count. I thought for a moment of telling him of the precious and pricey exotica I had savoured down in the swanky south – single-origin bars crafted by ascetic Danes for after-dinner connoisseurs, say, or tablets of Ecuadorian magic presented in teak cabinets – but then I got over myself and said: "Something dark. Bournville, say."

"Fair enough," said Lee. "That's from our Birmingham brethren, down south." Geoff and Joan spoke up for Dairy Milk. "Cadbury's too," Lee drily noted. "Fair do's to them. But they learned it all from York folk."

So indeed they had. Lee led us into a little auditorium furnished, bizarrely, with velvet-covered chaises longues, and then conjured speech from a series of talking three-dimensional portraits on the walls. He had his pattering interaction down to a fine art, and bantered back and forth with early Terrys and other chocolate pioneers in a manner which made light of their artificiality and educational script. It helped no end that, unlike at Cadbury World, the technology actually functioned.

Most significant among the talking heads was Mary Tuke, a York Quaker born in 1695 who in 1725 opened a shop on Walmgate in the centre of the city to sell groceries. At this time cocoa was sold as a solid mass, broken up into smaller 'cakes' that Mary and her fellow grocers sold by weight.

Mary passed her business on to her nephew William, who became a pioneer not only of chocolate manufacture but also in the treatment of mental health disorders. He set up a retreat 'for Persons Afflicted with Disorders of the Mind', which was one of Britain's first humane mental healthcare institutions.

By the 19th century the Tukes were not only producing but also packaging cocoa under their own brand, as 'Tuke's Superior Rock Cocoa', and in 1862 they decided to pass on the business to one of their managers, a young Quaker gentleman by the name of Henry Isaac Rowntree.

Rowntree was a man, the Tukes declared, 'whose knowledge of the business in its several departments enables us with confidence to recommend him to the notice of our connection'.

The Rowntree family had already had a profound effect on the history of chocolate in this country when a young man from another Quaker family served an apprenticeship at the Rowntree's grocery shop on the Pavement in York. This was George Cadbury, who would take what he had learned back to his own family business in Birmingham.

Henry Isaac Rowntree, meanwhile, rebranded Tuke's Rock Cocoa as Rowntree's, and a celebrated chocolate brand was born.

The combined business thrived – not without hiccups – and Henry's brother Joseph Rowntree built a vast factory on Haxby Road, outside the crowded ancient centre, in 1890. Perhaps they are most famous for fruit pastilles and fruit gums, but Rowntrees also developed one of Britain's best-loved boxes of soft-centred chocolates, Black Magic, the result of a pioneering process of market research by Peter Rowntree early in the 20th century (and the subject of dramatic television advertisements that are still spoofed to this day).

A later merger, with the toffee specialists Mackintosh in the 1960s, brought more cherished brands (including Rolo, Quality Street and Toffee Crisp) into the fold, but before long the continentals came calling and Rowntree Mackintosh was absorbed into the giant Swiss Nestlé combine in 1988.

Like their Quaker counterparts the Cadburys in Birmingham, the Rowntree family made enormous contributions to the social development of their city, building not only their factory but also an entire community at New Earswick.

This drew on the conclusions of the remarkable social studies conducted by Joseph's son Seebohm Rowntree, who interviewed more than 11,000 families at the very end of the 19th century in an attempt to understand the causes of poverty. His report and its conclusions would help to shape not only the new model community of York, but also the foundation of the welfare state in years to come.

> " He told us the date of introduction of our favourite bars, and our family's favourite bars and – this was clearly a favourite party trick – any bar or sort of British chocolate you cared to mention

All of this fascinating information – and a great deal more – was delivered by the jovial Lee as he conducted us around York's Chocolate Story. He rattled through the basics of chocolate cultivation, processing and manufacture, handing out Quality Street (very popular) and samples of 100% chocolate (much less so).

He told us the date of introduction of our favourite bars, and our family's favourite bars and – this was clearly a favourite party trick – any bar or sort of British chocolate you cared to mention, even if your favourite item in the entire chocolate world was a blue Smartie (1989, replacing the brown one; dropped in 2006 because of a hoo-ha about artificial colours; reintroduced with seaweed-derived colouring in 2008. Good grief!).

At his bidding, Geoff, Joan and I waggled assorted levers and twizzled wheels to mimic the chocolate production process, sat around a tasting table to discuss flavours and regional preferences, and eventually graduated to the kitchen end of things where we took our places at a workbench and were served up puddles of chocolate (white, rather disappointingly, and Belgian, rather than York-made) to form into giant lollipops and decorate with our choice of sugary decorations.

After that a nice young lady demonstrated in a lively and engaging manner the hand-manufacture of filled chocolates. Unlike her counterpart at Cadbury World she was not using ubiquitous Dairy Milk gunk but a decent (albeit continental) chocolate, and she actually filled these with an interesting mixture – a mango and white chocolate ganache, in fact.

A further advance over the Birmingham museum was that the smiley demonstrator was not obliged to wearily intone that her chocolate was for demonstration purposes only and not on any account to be tasted.

In fact she did the opposite and declared that not only were we most welcome to sample some mango chocolates that she had made earlier, but that – since we were coming to the end of the day and she was not expecting another large party – we would be doing her a great favour if we took as many as we liked, and filled a bag for our friends and families as well.

Talk about sending your audience away with a smile on their faces.

Delivered downstairs with a bumper bag of mango-ganache-filled milk chocolates and a feeling of warm benevolence towards all things York-chocolate-related, I turned right out of the up-to-date Chocolate Story building and walked 10 steps down the road – and into the 15th century.

The Shambles is York's most entirely intact ancient shopping street, a thoroughfare that, in a city of charming locations, ticks every box for the would-be time traveller.

It is sometimes difficult, in the country that is home to the Harry Potter Studio Experience, Bicester Shopping Village and the London Dungeon, to believe that an entirely convincing olde worlde scene is in fact the real thing and not something knocked up by the tourist board with a laptop, a 3D printer and some glue.

The Shambles, though, is absolutely genuine. It is true that its primary function has diverged some way from its former role as the focal point of the city's butchery trade – as recently as the late 19th century there were more than 25 butchers on this single, narrow street – and the deep gutters no longer run with blood, thank heavens.

> **York, with its wonderful combination of ancient and attractive buildings, chocolate heritage and curious and affluent customers, is the perfect place to make that kind of project viable**

But the buildings, most of them pre-dating Shakespeare and Good Queen Bess, are original and remarkably un-messed-around. The chop and sausage mongers have been replaced by traders with a distinct bias towards the crystal, the occult and the spuriously ancient, but there is a fudge shoppe and – most significantly for our purposes – a charming little chocolate shoppe, where many of the wares on sale are made on the premises.

This is Monk Bar Chocolatiers, a most inviting little enterprise. Of course, it helps that the exterior looks like one of the smaller and cuter potion shops in Diagon Alley, and the tiny interior is cosy and atmospheric. But this is also an entirely functional chocolate shop and – all the more impressive, given the space constraints – chocolate manufactory, where Ray Cardy and his son Alan hand-make small batches of shaped and filled chocolates using first-rate bought-in materials.

Whoever is not on making duty serves behind the counter, and on my visit I discovered Alan discussing the virtues of some of their favourite fillings (there are 60 or so on regular offer) with a customer who clearly had in-depth knowledge of most of the range.

There are single-origin bars as well as soft centres and shaped singles: I scored a bag of Belgian milk hearts, which kept me going very nicely on the short walk to my next destination. But before I set off I paused for a selfie in front of Britain's most picturesque little chocolate shop.

I resisted the impulse to dart down the alleyways that run off to either side of the Shambles (they are called snickelways and they are very intriguing) and headed downhill to the bottom. Right turn, along another charming pedestrian thoroughfare (even Nando's looks alluringly ancient) and up another quiet side street is the York Cocoa Works, where I was due to be taught a lesson.

York Cocoa Works evolved from York Cocoa House, a picturesque chocolate shop, chocolate maker and tea shop close to York Minster.

The workshop is a more expansive set-up, and the most satisfying expression so far of the cocoa-related dreams of Sophie Jewett.

Sophie is a very good example of the kind of person who inspired this book — a lifelong chocolate enthusiast with the dedication, drive and energy to convey her love for the bean and all that comes from it to the widest possible audience.

York, with its wonderful combination of ancient and attractive buildings, chocolate heritage and curious and affluent customers, is the perfect place to make that kind of project viable. And what a project it is.

At the workshop you can buy chocolates and eat chocolates (and other lovely things) and wash them down with hot chocolate. But you can also, through the plate-glass windows that give on to some impressively vast machinery, watch every stage of the transformation of cocoa beans into delicious finished items.

This is what is missing at Cadbury World, and also missing from the laudable Chocolate Story up the road. Large-scale chocolate factories making quality chocolate, such as Hotel Chocolat's vast and fascinating set-up in Huntingdon, necessarily exclude the public.

But Sophie Jewett has brought the whole process centre stage in the most remarkable manner. And it took a bit of doing.

The Cocoa Works is ideally positioned, from a historical point of view, on Castlegate, no more than a Rolo's throw from the Tuke family's cocoa, chocolate and chicory workshop that Henry Isaac Rowntree took over in 1862. In chocolate terms, this is hallowed ground.

But this is not another olde worlde building. With huge plate-glass windows and bright-red brick it looks entirely 21st century and up to date, no doubt reassuring for the clients of Jobcentre Plus which occupied the building before Sophie started to move in her machinery.

That in itself was no straightforward task. "The biggest machine made it through the space by barely an inch," she recalls. "I couldn't watch."

But all that heavy lifting was worth it, because customers supping their hot chocolate can now observe a longitudinal conch at work, and a number of other equally substantial and impressive bits of kit, and be guaranteed a lucid explanation of what is going on from the person who served them their cocoa.

"Better not get me started on the longitudinal conch," Sophie warned. "That's what I really wanted. It combines an antique structure with modern engineering. I stroke it from time to time, when I think nobody's watching."

The beauty of the little factory's street-corner location and extensive glazing is that all kinds of people might actually be watching Sophie caress her machinery, not only through the internal windows giving on to the cafe, but also through the two huge shop windows facing out to the street. It seems unlikely that she will object to the attention.

Sophie set up her first chocolate shop on Blake Street, close to York Minster, in 2011, but chocolate had been on her mind for much longer than that.

"I started making cakes when I was four," she said, taking a sip of cocoa. "By the age of eight I had my own signature chocolate fudge recipe; when I was 12 my school project was to track the Cadbury share price, then that Easter I taught myself how to temper chocolate. I realised a few years ago that I was quite obsessed, so I launched my own chocolate-making business – Little Pretty Things – making chocolates in my own home and teaching in people's kitchens. In September 2011 we discovered the perfect location for us, and the Cocoa House started writing its own story."

She had recognised the huge power of chocolate in the city – the way that everyone seemed to have a relative or friend or ancestor who had worked with chocolate, and a love for the substance and the heritage that goes with it.

"When we held the York Chocolate Festival in 2012, the reaction from people was amazing," she recalled. "This was a city not only of Romans and Vikings and railways, but of chocolate as well." She and her team have been tapping into this enthusiasm ever since.

The shop on Blake Street was always crammed with customers – locals as well as tourists – but had limited scope to function as a chocolate-making facility as well as a chocolate-serving facility, with truffles being rolled on marble slabs even as pots of tea and slices of cake were delivered to tables.

So that shop has, reluctantly, been left behind, and the workshop offers a much more ambitious range of activities – as well as lovely hot chocolate and baked goods.

In addition to producing sophisticated, small-batch chocolate from responsibly sourced beans, which sit in bulging stacks on the factory floor, the smart teaching space offers room to instruct a dozen would-be chocolatiers at a time.

> " I started making cakes when I was four," she said, taking a sip of cocoa. "By the age of eight I had my own signature chocolate fudge recipe; when I was 12 my school project was to track the Cadbury share price, then that Easter I taught myself how to temper chocolate

By way of a hands-on demonstration, Sophie picked up a steel bowl and started to melt cubes of 63% Colombian chocolate over hot water. Once the edges had softened and the mass had started to deliquesce, she handed me the bowl, spoon and a hairdryer.

"Keep going with that for a while," she suggested. "We'll temper it in a minute."

Tempering is one of the key techniques in chocolate manufacture. I never tire of watching it being done by a professional, and it's always fun to have a go myself.

The process consists of working melted chocolate on a smooth, cool surface so that the chocolate itself cools and its chemical structure changes, ensuring a finished product that is smooth and even in texture and glossy in appearance.

Watching Sophie pour a vast puddle of dark chocolate onto a marble slab and then sweep it back and forth with confident arcs of a palette knife was a tremendously satisfying experience. Trying to mimic her actions was rather less so, and startling quantities of chocolate ended up on my apron rather than on the table.

Still... "Not bad," she concluded, as I shamelessly licked my fingers. "You've got potential."

I doubt it. But for anyone who has, the Cocoa Works is an ideal place to hone their skills. Sophie and her fellow experts – she works with eight chocolate makers at present – are happy to take on absolute beginners, or welcome more serious amateurs to longer, skill-specific workshops.

But more than that, Sophie is committed to making this a centre for every kind of chocolate enthusiast, even those who might one day turn out to be commercial rivals. She is willing to help people not only hone their skills but develop products, and decide which raw materials are best for their plans.

It is an inspiring combination of altruism and enthusiasm, but also reflects her deeply held belief that a healthier, more respectful and less impatient relationship with food will be beneficial not only to the inhabitants of York but to mankind in general.

"We really need to change people's behaviour," she declared. "It's interesting that cookery programmes of all sorts – *Masterchef, Bake Off* and so on – pull in the very top ratings on television, but a lot of people aren't actually cooking for themselves any more." They are watching other people cook, while eating something that they ordered in from Deliveroo or Uber Eats. It's a miserable prospect for the future.

One that Sophie is determined to change. "That's what this space is about," she said, scooping the tempered chocolate back into the bowl, ready to be used in another of her constant flavour experiments.

"We want to give people a space where they can come and learn the skills, and get actively involved in the things that they eat."

The good news is that the future for chocolate in the lovely city of York seems to be very bright, and the better news for those of us unlucky enough not to live there is that Sophie is not alone.

Not all that far away, and still in God's own county, similar stirrings are occurring in the great steel city of Sheffield. Fittingly, there is a metallic theme.

Sheffield is not, on the face of it, so attractive a city as York. It may be built, like Rome, on seven hills, but there are precious few Roman remains to be seen – and you may find it hard to find anyone who can identify with any certainty all of those seven hills.

But it is a bright and lively city nonetheless, with plenty of more recent heritage and a thriving and youthful population with a healthy regard for good food and drink. All of which makes it a promising spot for an entrepreneur with a taste for chocolate to seek to make his fortune. And Max Scotford seems to have had Sheffield's metal-bashing identity as the Steel City in mind when he chose the name Bullion for his chocolate company. Not so. In fact, his inspiration was far away and a long, long time ago...

"The name was inspired by the Mayan Indians of Central America," Max explained. "Round about 600AD they were making a chocolate drink by roasting the cocoa beans and adding water and spices. They valued this drink so highly that they came to use cocoa beans as a form of currency."

Max also sets great value by fine cocoa beans, so he thought to name the bars that were made from them after precious metal – and the Bullion brand was born. The name also gives him the opportunity to clothe his wares in shiny golden wrappers, but once these come off, a first-rate slab of bean-to-bar goodness is revealed.

Bullion bars have been well received by public and expert judges alike, picking up healthy sales through the usual bean-to-bar network and a clutch of medals at national and international competitions.

But Max has greater ambitions in mind. Like Sophie Jewett in York, he enjoys seeing people's reactions when they take their first taste of his bars. "Witnessing someone taste true craft chocolate for the first time is quite special for me," he said. "Something they thought they knew, but they actually really didn't. It only takes a bite to realise that."

He wants to raise a generation of chocolate connoisseurs in Sheffield, and give them a place where they can taste and learn about great chocolate, and discuss what they have discovered.

"Just as with fine wine, we want people to discuss the origin and flavour notes of the chocolate we produce," he said.

So he has raised more than £10,000 on Kickstarter to open a chocolate-themed cafe in the Cutlery Hall alongside Bullion's new bean-to-bar chocolate factory at Kelham Island.

The island is well worth a visit even for the chocolate sceptic. It was man-made for industrial purposes (well, to power a watermill) in Norman times and later served as the centre of Sheffield's world-famous steel and cutlery industries. Some relics of heavy industry remain, among them a Bessemer converter and Europe's largest working steam engine.

But it also celebrates the city's food and drink history, most notably Sheffield's long and proud brewing tradition. There are half a dozen first-rate alehouses in the area, and around them has gathered a gaggle of fine eateries. Max plans to add chocolate-related snacks to the local foodies' menus, and single-origin bars to their shopping lists.

It took less than a month to raise the money to build the cafe from a huge range of small donors, which suggests that there is plenty of as-yet-unsatisfied enthusiasm in the city for top-quality chocolate. And judging by the success that Sophie Jewett has made of her similar venture in York, the future for Bullion looks shiny bright.

□ To educate your chocolate palate in a most enjoyable way, I suggest buying a range of Cocoa House little bars at 63% strength: it depends what is in stock, which depends in turn on what high-quality beans Sophie has been able to source at the time of your visit – but if you get the chance, try comparing a 63% bar made with beans from Kerala in India with one from Peru, one from Colombia and one from Uganda (the Mountains of the Moon cacao is terrific). You should be able to detect clear differences between each, and the experience is just what the Cocoa House is all about.

□ In York, go to Monk Bar Chocolatiers to take your selfies, and buy a little bag of Belgian chocolate hearts or truffles to pose with. But save up to buy your real treats at York Cocoa House.

TASTING NOTES

□ If you wish to evoke the memory of a Terry's Chocolate Orange far more effectively than today's feeble imitation that wears its name, treat yourself to a packet of the Cocoa House's chocolate orange buttons, which are low on sugar but high on delicious fruit flavour: £5.

□ Bullion's single-origin bars are terrific. The current range uses cacao from Haiti, Bolivia and Guatemala. My favourite is the Bolivian Alto Beni 70%, with flavour notes of malt and green olives. It's £7.95.

WHAT IS BEAN TO BAR?

It's the title of this book, which suggests that it has a certain importance, to my mind. 'Bean to bar' is the process by which careful makers produce their chocolate and it has become a kind of shorthand for the entire artisanal chocolate industry that is happily thriving around the world, and creating so much contentment among creators and consumers in Britain.

The bean-to-bar movement emerged in the United States towards the end of the last century. In her excellent book on the topic, the US chocolate expert Megan Giller (who blogs at megangiller.com – highly recommended) suggests that the very first exponents were Scharffen Berger of the Bay Area in Northern California. In 1996, Robert Steinberg and John Scharffenberger thought it would be an enjoyable hobby to make bars of chocolate from scratch.

In the process they started a revolution in engaged food production – and they also coined the phrase for what they were doing: making chocolate 'from bean to bar'.

Scharffen Berger quickly won a host of admirers and – more gradually – some accomplished imitators. I would love to say that their story continues to this day and that they are still producing chocolate in the same romantic way. But, in fact, the founders received an offer they couldn't refuse in 2005 from the giant and ghastly Hershey Company, who bought the company, moved it to Illinois – and changed the method of chocolate making.

But the genie was out of the bottle by then, and the method and philosophy of making chocolate from bean to bar caught on and has been catching on ever since.

It's self-explanatory really, but I'll expand for clarity. Giant confectionery companies buy their beans in bulk, often with little knowledge of precisely where the beans have come from. They sometimes acquire their chocolate in the form of pre-prepared 'cocoa mass' shipped in tankers.

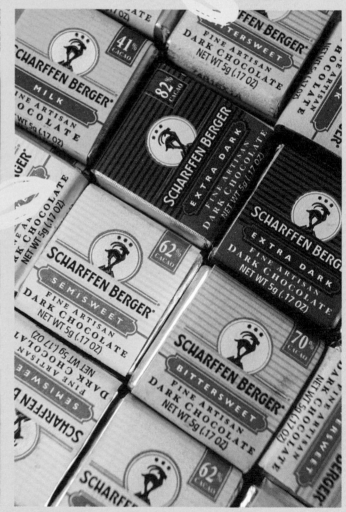

They add colossal quantities of sugar, cheap fat, flavourings and emulsifiers such as soya lecithin, which renders the flavour and texture 'consistent'. This is industrial chocolate.

Bean-to-bar makers are properly, intimately involved in every stage of the production of their chocolate. They acquire their beans in small quantities, often direct from the growers or from specialist importers who know where the beans were grown, under what conditions, and by whom.

They pay not just the Fairtrade price trumpeted by multinationals (no bad thing) but often many times more than that – fair recompense for the farmers' work. Makers often visit plantations and forests to see the trees and meet the people tending them, gaining knowledge about growing conditions – and knowledge about the communities that the crop supports.

Bean-to-bar makers pay tremendous attention to the state of the beans that they are buying – sometimes, as we shall see, even studying the particular small patch of land where they grew, the other plants that surrounded the cacao trees, and their geographical orientation.

They will examine the beans before buying, paying attention to their physical condition and also their state of fermentation. When they get the beans back to their workshop, kitchen or factory they will check them over once more, removing twigs and other detritus, and any broken or mouldy beans, and roast them (unless they are making 'raw' chocolate – see Forever Cacao).

This kills bacteria and helps to develop the flavour in the same manner as roasting coffee beans – a light roast or a longer process can make a considerable difference to the eventual flavour of the chocolate. Roasting also helps to loosen shells for the next part of the process. This is crushing, which breaks away the papery shell and leaves the maker with shards of bean called nibs.

If you ever get the chance (and lots of bean-to-bar makers will have roasted beans on hand in their shops or on their stalls at markets and food fairs), you can crush a roasted bean between two fingers and pop the nibs into your mouth. It's a sharp, intense flavour, difficult to enjoy on its own, but nibs are often added as a garnish, and source of texture, to artisan bars.

Next is a stage called winnowing, sometimes achieved with the aid of a hairdryer, in which the shreds of outer shell are blown away, leaving just the nibs behind. Discarded shells need not go to waste. Brewed with freshly boiled water in a cafetiere, they make a powerfully chocolatey (but not at all sweet) infusion which is sometimes known as cacao tea or cocoa tea. Both Duffy's of Lincolnshire and Hotel Chocolat have produced delicious versions. I can't, however, recommend it as a soothing bedtime brew, as the theobromine in the cacao shells works not unlike caffeine or tannin in coffee or tea…

If not distracted by making cacao tea, the bean-to-bar chocolate maker pops the nibs into a grinder, which turns them into a paste known as 'cocoa liquor'. The action of the grinder also releases the cocoa butter that is naturally present in the nibs, which lubricates and loosens the liquor.

At this stage the artisan chocolate maker may add extra butter to the liquor, and, unless they are making a 100% bar, sugar.

The percentage figure that you often see on a bar of fine chocolate refers to the proportion of chocolate liquor and cocoa butter that the bar contains. Look at the other ingredients. If it's only sugar, than a bar of 70% dark chocolate contains 70% cocoa butter and chocolate liquor, and 30% sugar.

Milk solids and other flavours in powder form can also be added at this stage. But if it is a purist's bar, it will be just cocoa butter and sugar.

The next stage is called conching, and this mixes all the ingredients together, aerating the mixture and changing the texture and 'finish' — the shine or polish of the finished bar. Conching machines are essentially grinders, but makers can be very finickety about the mechanics and processes involved, and often become profoundly attached to individual machines.

Some well-equipped bean-to-bar makers have invested in a device called a melanger, which can both grind and conch.

Such machine mania may be one reason why bean-to-bar chocolate making has attracted a certain kind of engineering genius — for example, Duffy Sheardown and Willie Harcourt-Cooze — as well as those of a more culinary bent.

Not content with discussing the finer points of their machines, bean-to-bar makers spend a lot of time experimenting with different lengths of conch. With good reason – the difference in flavour and texture of the same mixture after 24 hours in the machine and after 48 hours can be quite remarkable.

Only one stage remains now before the chocolate is ready to eat. This is tempering, in which the conched chocolate mixture is heated and then cooled. This renders it stable, so that it will have a decent shelf-life (many months, if properly kept), and also gives the chocolate a lovely sheen and a healthy 'snap' when a bar is broken. A soft or over-brittle snap, or swirls or bubbles on the surface, are all signs of an ill-tempered bar (and likely to provoke ill temper in the person who made it).

Tempering in the classical, small-scale manner is performed by pouring the molten chocolate onto a cool slab of marble (the process in which I 'assisted' Sophie Jewett at York Cocoa Works). This cools the chocolate quickly and evenly, and the chocolate maker smooths and scoops the mixture over the stone until the desired texture is reached.

Obviously this can't be done by hand on a large scale, so bean-to-bar makers operating on even a modest basis usually get hold of a tempering machine, often a fairly basic device rather like a vertical record player, where the mixture coats a rotating disc and is scooped off it by a fixed blade. I can watch this happen for hours.

Some chocolate makers age their cooled chocolate in large containers between conching and tempering. Others experiment at this stage by storing chocolate blocks in ways that may impart flavour, such as in barrels previously used to store brandy or whisky.

But the chocolate is ready for use after tempering and can be poured into moulds to make bars, used to 'enrobe' fillings for filled chocolates, mixed with cream or other liquids to make a ganache or truffle, or employed for whatever other debauched purpose the human mind can concoct.

Needless to say, there are as many variations on the bean-to-bar process as there are makers of chocolate. A few makers – notably, in this country, Forever Cacao in Wales – believe that roasting beans is unnecessary and introduces an impediment between farmer and consumer. If you see a bar that announces it is 'raw' chocolate, that means the beans have not been roasted. Since, whatever else roasting may achieve, it certainly kills bacteria, some people (and indeed the health authorities in some countries) believe that there may be health risks associated with the consumption of raw chocolate, particularly by the very young, the very old or those in delicate health. I am not qualified to comment on this, but thought I should mention it. I have eaten raw chocolate on a number of occasions, with no effect other than the improved sense of general wellbeing that I get from good chocolate of any kind.

Every maker will have their own theories about the optimum roasting and/or conching times for particular types of bean. Others will ask their growers to pursue a particular timescale or method in the fermentation of beans after harvest.

This last measure is easier to achieve for those makers who can call themselves 'tree-to-bar' since they control every aspect of production from harvest through to the final moulding of the bars. Hotel Chocolat can do this, for example, with chocolate made from beans grown on the plantation in St Lucia.

Other interesting exponents of 'tree-to-bar' making have chocolate factories close to the plantations themselves. For obvious reasons none of these makers are British (you can't grow chocolate in the UK), but British consumers can check out Madagascan-made bars sold here by MIA (Made in Africa) and imported bars from the likes of Menakao (also Madagascan), Marou in Vietnam, my determined and passionate friend Susana Cardenas in Ecuador and the brilliant Luisa Abram in Brazil.

When you have explored all the wonderful creations made by British bean-to-bar makers, you could take an enjoyable international break by exploring the wilder fringes of the international tree-to-bar brigade. London's own Cocoa Runners (cocoarunners.com) will be delighted to help you discover them, and more…

THE EAST

FULL OF CHOCOLATE PROMISE

USEFUL INFO

Cleethorpes station is practically on the beach. Direct trains from Manchester Piccadilly take about 2.75 hours. Trains from London King's Cross take about 3.5 hours with a change at Doncaster.

By car: Come off the A1 (M) onto the M18 near Doncaster, then onto the M180 to Grimsby and Cleethorpes.

Duffy's factory is at **Unit 2E, Humberston Business Park, Wilton Road, Humberston, DN36 4BJ** Please don't just drop in unannounced. Consult his website at **duffyschocolate.co.uk** or follow him on Facebook for details of open days, masterclasses, messy sessions for children, etc.

The same applies to **Emily Robertson** in Caistor – it's a lovely little town, on the A46 and roughly equidistant from Lincoln and Cleethorpes, but Emily is busy so it is best to buy her bars online (see Tasting Notes).

Pump Street Bakery, **1 Pump Street, Orford, Woodbridge, IP12 2LZ**

By car: Orford is quite a long way east of the A12, which runs from Ipswich to Lowestoft

By train/bus: A train from Liverpool Street Station in London to Woodbridge (Suffolk) will take about 90 minutes, then go by taxi to Orford, which should cost in the region of £20–£25. There are buses, but not many of them.

Open: Tue–Sat 9am–4pm (on Tue, takeaway only); Sun 10am–4pm. For specific dates and further details, check the website at **pumpstreetchocolate.com**

Lincoln is comparatively easy to access, via the A1 and then the A46, or by train, changing from the mainline at Newark Northgate on to an endearing little trundler that will take you into Lincoln Central in 20 minutes. So it's easy to get there, but unfortunately there's not much in the way of chocolate when you arrive. The fudge shop is awesome, though. Oh, and the cathedral's pretty good, too.

THE GENIUS
OF CLEETHORPES

Those raised on Roald Dahl or cinematic versions of his work may
have unrealistic notions of what a chocolate factory should look
like, and where it might be located. Willy Wonka's workplace looms
over the surrounding houses like a Brutalist power station, while
the interior is a candy-coloured playground for Oompa-Loompas.

Real life, it may be a relief to discover, is not like that. The sprawling Cadbury
complex in Birmingham is startling in scale, and Hotel Chocolat's ultra-modern
edifice in Huntingdon is startling in its technological advancement, but some
of the finest chocolate made in this country comes from the most modest
of premises.

And perhaps the greatest contrast between sophistication of product and place of
manufacture arises with Duffy's – which may well be the loveliest and most refined
chocolate bars that the UK produces, and which emerge from a small industrial
unit in Humberston, on the outskirts of Cleethorpes.

This is a lengthy pilgrimage from almost anywhere else in the UK, and those who
set out to visit it should plan in advance to coincide with a masterclass, a tasting
or (depending on the age of your dependants), a messy youth-oriented exploration
session. All of these are on offer, but most of the time Gerald 'Duffy' Sheardown
contents himself with the serious production of seriously beautiful chocolate.

I learned a long time ago that there is no such thing as a typical chocolate maker, but Duffy is unusual even by the standards of this unorthodox breed.

People often come to chocolate through an interest in other foods and an aptitude for flavour combinations, and then find themselves expensively baffled the first time that their machinery breaks down. But Duffy arrived in the world of chocolate via a lengthy and distinguished career in a more mechanical environment, as a motor-racing engineer.

He fettled cars for some of the world's finest drivers (among them perhaps the greatest of all, Ayrton Senna) and had countless adventures in the pit lanes of racetracks all over the world. It was a lot of fun, he readily concedes, but it took him too often away from home and from his beloved wife Penny.

On a rare visit home the two were listening to Radio Four one day and heard a food programme which included the assertion that Cadbury was the only company in the UK to make chocolate 'from bean to bar' (this was some time ago – happily, as we have seen, that is no longer the case). Anyhow, Duffy said to himself "I can do that", and his second career was born.

This was more than a decade ago – a time when chocolate-making machinery was bulkier, more expensive and more prone to breakage than it is now. But motor racing breeds mechanical improvisation, and Duffy is very much at home with a spanner in one hand and a bit of recalcitrant metal in the other, and soon he had his equipment up and running and turned to the other vital element in the manufacture of fine chocolate – sourcing a supply of good cacao beans.

Duffy put in the hard yards, travelling to food fairs and sampling small quantities of exotic beans, making contacts and eventually tracking down the suppliers who could match his exacting standards.

As he points out, his new career was not, in essence, all that different from his previous one. "They both involve long hours, technical rigour, hard work and passion." And, he might add, the dedicated pursuit of excellence.

Every time he visited the racetrack it was with the intention of seeing his car first past the chequered flag. And when it came to making chocolate, he wanted to make the best in the world.

He succeeded. And you needn't just take my word for it. The Academy of Chocolate in London awarded Duffy its Golden Bean for the best bar of chocolate of the year in 2011 for his Indio Rojo, made with beans from Honduras, a bar that he still makes, subject to availability of the vital beans.

When I am asked to identify my favourite bar of chocolate in the world (and I am, usually by people whose Galaxy I have pooh-poohed), I nominate Duffy's Venezuela Ocumare 72%, made with the much-prized Criollo beans that arc, according to Duffy, "fiddly to work with but well worth the effort".

These are just two from a range that varies according to the beans that Duffy can get hold of, but almost always features his best-sellers and boasts a variety of percentages and additions. Duffy's bars are widely available in specialist chocolate shops and online, but you may also come across his chocolate without knowing it – Duffy's creations are often used as raw material by makers of fine filled chocolate and by chef-patissiers.

But the best way to get your hands on a bar of Duffy's is to venture up to Cleethorpes and meet the man himself at a tasting. That way you benefit from some friendly tuition, excellent hospitality and an inexhaustible fund of stories.

Some people might worry that those who are serious about good chocolate might be serious about how to use it – and too serious to enjoy it. Duffy is the antidote to any such ideas. He does make very lovely bars, but he also loves messing around with chocolate, and he is very much in favour of introducing people to the delights of chocolate by way of letting them manufacture outrageous creations using his raw materials.

His adults-only 'messy' sessions in the chocolate studio at the Cleethorpes factory are everything that the title promises, and participants often end up with as much chocolate on their clothing as in their finished bars, which can be adorned with such resolutely unserious decorations as sugar sprinkles. But participants also get a reasonable grasp of how Duffy makes the good stuff, and he throws in a truffle-making lesson as well.

Cleethorpes itself may not be the most glamorous of English seaside resorts – and that is, technically, not the sea that you are looking at from the shore, but the Humber Estuary – but there is a nice little fake castle, an excellent boating lake and a miniature railway, and you can walk off any excess chocolate consumption with a stroll along the fine, expansive (at low tide) and gently sloping beach.

Among the regular visitors (and an occasional co-host) at Duffy's tastings is Kathryn Laverack, who lives in the lovely town of Louth, nearby and inland a bit from Cleethorpes.

Kathryn is a dedicated fan of fine chocolate and compiles an excellent website on the topic as well as hosting a range of tastings and classes, often at Duffy's factory. One of her more imaginative (and I think terrific) ideas is a combination of Book Club and Chocolate Tasting Club which pairs unusual bars of single-origin chocolate from around the world with literary titles of greater or lesser relevance – and invites participants to comment on their enjoyment (or otherwise) of each at a convivial evening discussion. It's a great format and it deserves to catch on.

If you are planning a chocolate-themed tour of the area you could well pencil in Louth as a worthwhile stopping-off point. It may not have the spectacular beach or miniature railway of Cleethorpes, but it has plenty else going for it – not least Spire Chocolates, who make their chocolates in Duffy's studio space in Humberston.

Lindsay Gardner is the moving spirit behind Spire. A chocolatier rather than a bean-to-bar chocolate maker, she learned the basics with Duffy but decided that her métier was sculpted chocolates – especially her beloved pralines – rather than specialist bars.

Accordingly, Lindsay ships in top-quality chocolate from Belgium – and with Duffy on hand as a quality controller, she can be sure that it really is top quality – which she then fashions into a series of endearing chocolate animals: a quizzical alpaca, a cute squirrel and a very fine figure of a white chocolate polar bear, named Roly.

This is the kind of thing that can set my teeth on edge, since it is often done cack-handedly with indifferent chocolate, but Lindsay has learnt her business in the right way, takes great care with her creations and is obviously working with materials and inspiration that she adores, so it works.

Her shop's name refers to Louth's most obvious landmark, the amazing spire of St James's Church (the tallest spire of any medieval church in the country), a startlingly elegant masterpiece of ancient engineering that towers over the town. Seen from afar it seems quite out of scale with the surrounding settlement – almost all of which can be seen from the tower if you have the energy to climb it (and if it is open between repairs).

Louth resident Kathryn Laverack is a discerning judge and reckons that Lindsay makes the finest filled chocolates in Lincolnshire (it is a big county). She also recommends Tertulia, a Louth 'chocolate house' that serves excellent hot chocolate in both milk and dark varieties. "Belgian," Kathryn notes, "but still fabulous."

> **Lindsay ships in top-quality chocolate from Belgium ... which she then fashions into a series of endearing chocolate animals: a quizzical alpaca, a cute squirrel and a very fine figure of a white chocolate polar bear, named Roly**

While on your chocolate tour of the east you might consider a brief stop in the wonderful city of Lincoln, to undertake a little strenuous exercise with a reward at both ends.

Like Cleethorpes and Louth, Lincoln is some way off the commonly beaten track, but seems all the more peculiar (and all the more special) because it is essentially a fully formed medieval city in the middle of nowhere with the accoutrements of a modern settlement (Marks & Spencer, train station, university) attached, but safely out of the way of the pretty bits.

If detouring here, get off your train (or park close to the station) and head (on foot) up the High Street, following signs for the cathedral. Pause at Hotel Chocolat (on the right) and arm yourself with a small bar of single-origin chocolate. Then resume your walk going straight on, through the medieval gate beside the Guildhall.

As you march on – now on a pedestrianised stretch called The Strait – you will notice the gradient increasing, and you may (depending on your level of fitness) begin to feel a slight shortness of breath and a tightening in the gluteus maximus.

Persevere. The road narrows again, and becomes Steep Hill, and the reason for the name is immediately apparent. As the angle becomes more dramatic, so the character of the roadside shops improves, chains and branches giving way to quirky independents – a shop selling instruments stripped from retired RAF aircraft, one specialising in carved and soft-toy animals, a nifty junk/antique emporium – and the charm factor increases. But it does not peak just yet, and neither does the road.

Past the Jew's House restaurant (first-rate food in one of the oldest inhabited townhouses in the country) the hill becomes no longer just testing but actually comically intense. Regular folk stop and smile and grimace and take a few breaths here. Athletes pause, and frown, and adjust their stride pattern. The next 100 yards is essentially a mountain covered in tarmac, sensibly forbidden to vehicular traffic (and senselessly tobogganned by students when it snows) and quite uniquely arduous.

But then the gradient eases just a little, the cathedral is just around the corner, and you can take your reward, either at the Wig & Mitre or Magna Carta pubs, at Imperial Teas (good coffee, too) or – my usual destination – at Roly's Fudge. I realise that this is marginally off-topic, and that the *Fudge-Lover's Guide to Britain* is at the moment just a delicious idea (my idea, by the way, copyright in the most bulletproof manner and TM) – but Roly's fine fudges are made on the premises, are utterly delicious, are often displayed fresh on the tray in the window and – this is for me the clincher – the range includes a best-selling chocolate fudge that is made with dark chocolate and tastes of chocolate... as well as fudge.

Thus fortified, I recommend a wander around the cathedral, which is not only mind-boggling but contains an actual Magna Carta as well, before the infinitely easier descent to your starting point.

> **One stage in particular of the chocolate-making process – a stage that consumers very rarely think about – has a great deal in common with the production of bread, and sourdough bread in particular**

You'll pass a chocolate shop on your way down the hill, but while I wish the proprietor nothing but the best it is hard to recommend that you stop by. The owner drives every month or so to Belgium, where he bulk-buys filled chocolates of no great distinction. I don't know why he does this – perhaps he likes driving – because he could find much better chocolates much closer to home, and if they were marginally more expensive he would more than save the difference on petrol.

The only bars that he sells come from Montezuma's in Sussex far to the south, good enough in their own way and ethically fine. But in a decade as a chocolate-shop proprietor he had never heard of Duffy Sheardown, who – as we have seen – makes bars which are in their own way world famous, 20 miles up the road. I wished the chap well and recommended that he look up Duffy's online. But I wouldn't bet that he will.

If you are wise you will, as I did, stock up with vast quantities of fudge for the road, for journeys in Eastern England can take rather longer than those in more motorway-penetrated parts of Britain. It is best to relax, enjoy the scenery (it is not, whatever Noël Coward may have believed, all flat) and stop frequently for snacks.

Set your satnav (or hitch – good luck with trains and buses) for Orford, for there you will find not only the best Ness this side of Hadrian's Wall but also an excellent castle and Pump Street Bakery. The latter is just what its name suggests but this is not another fudge-style diversion, because as well as first-rate bread, the bakery in Orford makes some of the finest chocolate to be found anywhere on this island, and it is very much worth the lengthy detour required from almost any sensible route in order to find it.

It's not unusual to find coffee and chocolate in close company. As well as their physical similarity and a crossover in growing locations, the two beans are treated in a broadly similar fashion to release their goodness, and the flavours combine well in a multitude of formats. It seems natural that as well as offering (often indifferent) hot chocolate alongside their macchiatos, Americanos and espressos, high-street coffee chains should offer bars of chocolate. These are not always first rate, but we make an exception for the little bars of Willie's Cacao that are a near-irresistible impulse buy for me at the counter in Caffè Nero.

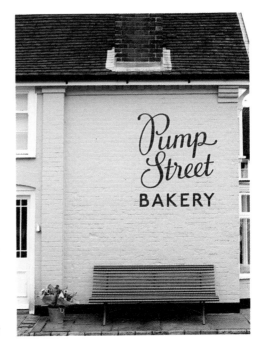

All of that makes sense. But a high-end bean-to-bar chocolate operation on the same premises as a high-end, top-quality bakery? In deepest East Anglia? That requires a little more explanation.

Yet according to Chris Brennan, who founded Pump Street Bakery in the village of Orford about eight years ago, the two products go together very well and have many affinities.

One stage in particular of the chocolate-making process – a stage that consumers very rarely think about – has a great deal in common with the production of bread, and sourdough bread in particular.

That stage is fermentation, which is the first process performed on cacao beans after harvesting – traditionally in piles of pods under banana leaves, but often now in purpose-built 'sweatboxes'. It is the first step on the way to determining the final flavour of the chocolate that will be produced from the beans once they have been further processed.

So for Brennan, making chocolate was a natural progression of sorts from the baking of bread – which is something that he came to in 'retirement' from a long and successful international career with the technology giant IBM.

Chris set up the bakery with his daughter Joanna, and just as his initial mild curiosity about the process of sourdough breadmaking turned into a determined process of research into the very best ingredients and processes for that food, so an interest in bean-to-bar chocolate turned into the pursuit of – you've guessed it – the very best ingredients and processes to manufacture the food of the gods.

The Brennans started to make chocolate in the pastry section of the bakery in 2012, and as their bars rapidly became a success, production was moved into an adjoining room in the old barn that housed the bakery.

Of course, there was an irresistible impulse to combine the two foods – and not in the way that some of us may associate with that messiest of childhood treats, chocolate spread on toast. And nothing to do with Nutella, either.

Obviously, the Pump Street approach required considerable experimentation, and Chris tried putting crumbs from the bakery's own sourdough loaves in with the beans from the village of Patanemo in Venezuela as he ground them, before adding sea salt.

The result is Pump Street's justly celebrated dark chocolate sourdough crumb and sea salt bar, now made with Hacienda Limon chocolate from Ecuador. It is one of my all-time favourite bars and one of the most moreish little slabs of fine chocolate that you will ever come across.

Pump Street sells its bars in sealed, padded envelopes – a typically practical and scientific method which protects the bar both in a physical sense and in the way that it preserves flavours. This means that when you break the seal on the sourdough crumb bar there is an instant burst of a wonderfully evocative bakery aroma with hints of dark chocolate behind it – as if one has been

transported for a moment from a workaday location to a warm and homely ancient bakery in a beautiful East Anglian village.

But that is just one of what is now quite a wide range of bars. Chris and Joanna take tremendous care in sourcing their suppliers – it can take as long as two years to locate the beans that they are after from a specific location – and then work hard with the farmers to try to ensure that the harvesting, fermenting and drying practices that they favour can be achieved.

Roasting, winnowing, grinding, conching and tempering are all undertaken by Chris, Joanna and their team, so this is a true bean-to-bar operation, and one that has justly won many awards not only in the UK but abroad as well.

But the chocolate manufacture no longer takes place in the old barn beside the bakery. As the reputation and sales of Pump Street's bars took off, it became clear that the original premises, attractive though they were, would not be fit for a larger operation. After an extensive search of the local area, the Brennans finally hit upon an unlikely solution – a building, disused for decades, that had once been used for keeping records of military vehicles and was adjacent to the large former fighter aircraft base at Bentwaters, not far from Orford.

So since 2017 the Pump Street team has been able to employ the same methods that they were using to make chocolate in the bakery, but with more equipment and a larger team. The idea has never been to make chocolate on a large scale, but rather to be able to make more small batches of fine chocolate at the same time.

It is heartening to see a lovely little business growing without losing sight of the passion with which it started. And clearly Chris and Joanna still love what they are doing.

"The job is as wonderful as it sounds," Joanna has said. "I like to try all of our chocolates, and other ones too, regularly to keep my palate calibrated." Keeping the palate calibrated – that's a good one, must remember that. All these empty wrappers under my desk? I'm just keeping my palate calibrated. It is not just the chocolate, though, according to Joanna, that keeps her happy at work. It's the people, too: "The amazing team we have in the bakery and in the chocolate factory – and the chance to delight people by offering them something really delicious."

You can share the joy by popping along to the bakery and tucking into the chocolate and bread. It is well worth the detour alone, but there are plenty of other reasons to head this way.

Orford is a pretty and fairly substantial village, and what is more it has a tremendous, unusual and unusually intact castle. The unique, massive polygonal keep is in very good nick and is these days under the care of English Heritage. Orford also has a rather marvellous and extremely photogenic lighthouse, decommissioned but preserved by a Trust on its own promontory and occasionally open for guided tours.

And there's more! Orford Ness is an extraordinary landscape dominated by a vast shingle spit. There is a nature reserve that plays host to a wonderful range of visiting birdlife, but fans of the weird will be more powerfully drawn by the array of sinister and strange concrete structures built by and for the armed forces. Many of these are still off limits for safety reasons, but their looming presence remains remarkably affecting for those of an imaginative frame of mind.

Not far along the coast is Aldeburgh, beloved of music lovers for its festivals associated with the music of Benjamin Britten, and Dunwich, or rather the remains of Dunwich, a medieval city of enormous size and importance (in its prime rivalling London in scale) which was swallowed by the sea hundreds of years ago after a series of dreadful storms.

They say that in stormy weather you can still hear the lost town's church bells tolling from the deep – but that is unfortunately complete cobblers. Notwithstanding such inventions, Dunwich is an evocative spot, and you'll have gathered that, all things considered, this chunk of the east coast is very much worth a visit.

> " Keeping the palate calibrated – that's a good one, must remember that. All these empty wrappers under my desk? I'm just keeping my palate calibrated

Inland again and back on the chocolate trail, the latest recruit to the ranks of eastern bean-to-bar makers is Emily Robertson, who founded Goldfinch Chocolate last year in the town of Caistor in Lincolnshire.

Caistor is a pleasant little community on the northern edge of the undulating Lincolnshire wolds. There are plenty of well-preserved Georgian and earlier buildings and a chunk of Roman wall (the town's name comes from the Latin *castrum*, meaning fortress, source of the English word castle).

Celebrities and significant moments in history are a little thin on the ground but the town is the supposed martyrdom site of one of Christ's apostles, Simon the Zealot, who according to local historians was crucified there on 10 May in AD 61, on the orders of a Roman procurator called Catus Decianus. The local historians seem admirably exact about the date, but they do admit that there are 'competing theories' as to the actual fate of Simon the Zealot, i.e the whole tale may be bunkum.

Anyhow, we are not here to debate apostolic demises, but to talk chocolate. Young Emily does all the work of chocolate manufacture by herself at home – making the chocolate bean to bar from scratch, designing and making the packaging, and running the website and the all-important social media outlets. It's a lot of work, but she is committed.

"I love chocolate and find the whole process of sourcing beans, tasting their differences, trying out different roasting profiles, inventing new recipes and experimenting with new ingredients so fun and interesting," Emily told me.

"I just find it so fascinating to discover the different tastes you can get from the cacao beans by changing or tweaking small aspects of the roasting and grinding, and to experiment with all the different tastes of beans which have been grown in different countries by different farmers."

Travelling around talking to chocolate makers who are just starting out, I have found a tremendous sense of camaraderie. Even though they are often working many miles from their nearest fellow craftsperson, the makers keep in constant touch on social media and compare notes at the fairs and festivals where they all go to sell what they have made.

Emily is no exception. "I've found over the past year and a half that the chocolate-making community has been extremely supportive," she said. "It's full of wonderfully enthusiastic people, willing to share knowledge and help with things from moral support to sourcing beans."

Like Solkiki down in Dorset, she uses coconut milk instead of dairy so that all of her bars are vegan. Working on a small scale, Emily can't produce bars from a wide variety of origins at the same time, instead ringing the changes with different flavours – a dark bar with beetroot, for example, and a coconut milk chocolate with roasted peanuts and smoked salt. That excellent creation won a Great Taste Award last year, a thrill for its young creator: "That was so encouraging. It was the first – and so far only – awards I had entered."

There will be more.

□ I have often gone on record to the effect that Duffy Sheardown is one of my favourite bean-to-bar makers on the planet, let alone in Britain, so I can do little more than beg you to get onto his website (duffyschocolate.co.uk) without delay and work your way through his range. If one or two bars are out of stock, you can also try the excellent and reliable cocoarunners.com.

□ If you prefer to buy your bars in person, hooray and good for you. Paul A Young usually has the entire Duffy's range in his lovely shops, and I have also seen Duffy's bars at Dormouse in Manchester and at the York Cocoa House.

□ One other point worthy of note is that Duffy's prices are notably reasonable – £6.95 at the top of the range and £5.65 for bars made with beans that are marginally easier to source. That is half the price of bars of similar, and often inferior, quality made by certain well-known European companies that shall remain nameless.

TASTING NOTES

□ If you have friends who remain stubbornly keen on Crapbury and similar, buy Duffy's Panama Tierra Oscura 40% (£5.65) and get them to blind-taste it next to Dairy Milk or Galaxy. You should win some easy converts.

□ Now – which is my favourite? Despite the wide selection this is actually quite an easy choice because Duffy's Venezuela Ocumare 72% is my go-to choice for consistently excellent dark chocolate. It has been one of my favourite bars for years and I see no reason to change my allegiance now. His 55% Venezuela Ocumare is a devastatingly good dark milk. They are both extraordinary value at £6.95.

☐ Pump Street's bars are fairly widely available – obviously on their own website (pumpstreetchocolate.com), via cocoarunners.com and from good chocolate retailers – for instance Sourced Market in London. But the best thing to do is to make a day of it and get along to the bakery itself in Orford – it's a lovely village with a quality castle and in the shop you will be able to talk to those who make the chocolate (and the bread, which is great), taste some of both, and no doubt buy plenty as well.

☐ Pump Street's range changes according to which beans they have been able to source, but you should always find a variation on their trademark bar which blends top-quality single-origin chocolate with rye or sourdough crumb and locally sourced sea salt.

☐ As I write I am nibbling on chunks of 60% Hacienda Limon from Ecuador with rye crumb and sea salt, and a more moreish creation it is difficult to imagine. It's £6.25, like most of their 70g bars.

Pump Street also does mini-bars, and they have a Rare Batch subscription club for limited-edition bars, which is a great way to broaden your palate.

☐ Availability of beans applies even more strongly to small-scale bean-to-bar makers who are just starting out, and who often source their beans one sack at a time. Do give Goldfinch Chocolate a go – find them on Facebook and see what Emily has been making. I've enjoyed a number of her bars made with beans from Belize, especially the award-winning 49% with peanut, and she does an excellent toasted white along the same lines as the much-garlanded Dormouse version. Emily has also been making bars with cacao from India, an increasingly popular source among bean-to-bar makers and well worth checking out.

☐ Pump Street will be running chocolate tours from summer 2019. The tours are £25 per person, which includes a voucher for a coffee at the bakery and a free chocolate bar. Children must be over 12 to attend, and all attendees must wear protective clothing.

WHERE DOES CHOCOLATE COME FROM?

I don't mean the bars. As this book laboriously sets out to prove, they come from Cleethorpes. And elsewhere in Britain. But where do the raw materials come from? Where do cacao beans grow?

On a surprisingly limited area of the planet, is the short answer: within a belt, or girdle, or band, around the Equator and 20 degrees either side of it.

If that is somewhat difficult to picture geographically, there are locational hints: Mexico is towards the extreme northern boundary, for example, and Madagascar towards its southern edge, which also brushes the 'top end' of Australia.

Entirely excluded are the mainland United States (although Hawaii is in) and all of Europe (though food historians note that Belgium's supposed excellence in chocolate production is linked to that country's vast former colonies in Africa).

Simply being within the equatorial band does not guarantee good growing conditions for cacao – soil type is also important. Cacao trees do not thrive in an alkaline soil, which explains why the crop does not do well on islands in the Caribbean where the soil is derived from coral (such as Barbados), while getting on beautifully on islands where it is not (St Lucia, Grenada).

The tree from which all chocolate is ultimately derived, *Theobroma cacao*, is a strange and fussy entity. The flowers and fruit (cocoa pods) grow directly from the trunk of the tree, which looks very strange indeed, and the trees themselves are picky about where they will flourish.

The pods tend not to fall from the tree, even when fully ripe, but must be harvested by hand by knowledgeable farmers who can tell when they are ready. This judgement can be aided by colour – immature pods come in

a wide variety of colours, but as they mature the pods often turn yellow or orange. Some makers contend that there can be a noticeable difference in eventual chocolate flavour depending on the colour of the pod.

Cacao trees can grow as high as 15 metres, but farmers prefer if possible to limit them to four or five metres for ease of harvesting. Pods can range from about 15cm to more than 35cm in length, and each one contains anything from 20 to 80 or so beans, embedded in white pulp.

There is great debate in chocolate circles about varieties of cacao and their different qualities. If you want a really long and complex conversation, just ask a chocolate nerd: "So, how many varieties of cacao would you say there are?"

The (very) short answer is three: Criollo, Forastero and Trinitario. Criollo is the most precious: native to central America, difficult to grow and responsible for only 5% of worldwide production, it is also believed to produce the most flavourful and complex beans.

Forastero is the most common, probably originating in the Amazon but now grown widely in Africa and Brazil and making up around 80% of the world's cocoa production.

Trinitario is a natural hybrid of the other two that is thought to have occurred first in Trinidad in 1727, when Forastero trees that had been planted to replace Criollo wiped out in a hurricane crossbred with survivors. Trinitario is now widespread in the Caribbean and in Central America, and can make very good chocolate indeed.

That story about the supposed origins of Trinitario illustrates the fact that natural hybrids of cacao can occur, and probably do occur, fairly easily. As a result there can be cachet attached to plantations of supposedly 'pure' Criollo, and makers and growers, especially in Central and South America, are often fiercely proud and protective of such locations.

But the truth is that no one can truly know how entirely pure any one particular tree really is.

And it should also be pointed out that variety of bean is not in itself any guarantee of good chocolate: care in harvesting, fermentation, storage and transport can all greatly affect flavour, even before the beans are roasted and the makers get their hands on them.

And the skill of the chocolate maker is also obviously significant: it is possible to make excellent chocolate from Forastero beans, just as it is from Trinitario, and it is possible to make lousy chocolate from Criollo, sad though it is to report.

The most productive cacao plantations do not feature rows of trees in neat and uncluttered rows like an orchard or olive grove; instead, they grow best among other vegetation, particularly in the shade of taller trees. There is much lively debate among growers about the best companion plants and trees, but everyone agrees that it is a tricky old business.

Not nearly as tricky as trying to raise a cacao tree in the UK, though.

My friend and colleague Richard Murray is a distinguished newspaper lawyer who in his spare time is a great fan of quality chocolate; we often compare notes and share bars in the office when I should be writing libellous stories and he should be rendering them safe for publication.

Richard is also a keen and accomplished gardener with a lovely plot in Uckfield in Sussex, but his efforts to grow his own cacao (and ultimately make his own home-grown chocolate) have so far been frustrated.

"I did manage to grow half a dozen trees at home to a reasonable size, about a metre or so," Richard told me. "But they were very fragile.

"The leaves of the young tree are very thin and prone to drying out," he reported, "so they need constant humidity. But they are also very prone to temperature variations. If either the humidity or the temperature falls below what they need, even for a short period of time, the leaves quickly turn brown and drop off."

Richard kept his young trees in his kitchen for a while, where they provided an excellent talking point at the table, but they seemed to stop growing – they survived, but did not thrive.

He felt that perhaps they were not getting enough light, so he created a clear polythene tent inside his garden greenhouse, and put his trees in it, with electric heaters controlled by a thermostat, and with sustained high levels of humidity.

Such horticultural intensive care should surely have borne fruit… but we will never know, because, as Richard confessed, "at some point the electricity tripped out and they all died."

A sad end to a brave experiment. More substantial growing efforts have seen limited success – the Eden Project in Cornwall has managed to coax pods from the half-dozen or so cacao trees in its rainforest biome, but not in quantities from which chocolate can be made (Cornish chocolate makers Chocolarder, based nearby, are monitoring developments). And there are cacao trees in the hothouses at Kew Gardens in London.

As Richard found, both heat and humidity are prerequisites for successful cacao cultivation, and lush forest locations with reliably high rainfall seem most fruitful.

It seems likely that the earliest populations of *Theobroma cacao* grew up in Central and South America, from where the crop gradually spread, with human intervention, around the world. Today about 70% of the world's cacao comes from Africa, source of the bulk supplies employed by the mass-market manufacturers.

The location where the beans are grown is of great importance to bean-to-bar makers, who like to emphasise that their bars are from a 'single origin' to distinguish them from mass-market bars made from beans from any number of unspecified locations.

Stating that a bar is made with Madagascan beans, Vietnamese beans or Ecuadorian beans can also raise expectations among consumers about the kind of taste experience that they are about to enjoy – seasoned fans of good chocolate will expect a Madagascan bar to be redolent of red fruits, and one from Vietnam to have elements of citrus in the taste, but how far these 'national' characteristics should be pursued is a matter for debate among growers and consumers.

Judges for prestigious chocolate awards may wish to consider how well a particular single-origin bar expresses the flavours of its constituent cacao. "Mmm," they may muse, savouring a tiny chunk of a contender, "classic Indonesia." This often makes me wonder how chocolate makers are supposed to innovate if they are constantly supposed to be upholding the expected flavours, but no matter.

Location is a useful shorthand for flavour characteristics, and an excellent framework for tasting experiments. Chocolate educators, such as Kathryn Laverack and Jennifer Earle, often theme tastings around bars from a single location made by different chocolatiers employing different methods.

So chocolate fans can enjoy a taste safari around the temperate regions of the world without leaving the comfort of their home town, and while savouring flavours that were born in the tropical forests that flourish either side of the Equator they can dream that one day they may get to see cacao growing in the wild, and harvest their own pods.

It just won't be happening in Uckfield.

THE
SOUTH WEST

MARVELS OF MOOR, TOR AND COVE

USEFUL INFO

If you want to see more of **Willie Harcourt-Cooze's factory**, please don't try to visit: everyone there is extremely busy trying to make chocolate! Instead have a look at the videos on Willie's website (**williescacao.com/willies-world/willies-tv**) and also check out his regular video updates on Facebook. On one of them you may well see me falling over a conching machine as I try to stay out of the way.

The bars and caramels are available at a wide range of retail outlets in the UK (and indeed all over the world). Notably in this country: Waitrose, Sainsbury's, Booths, Ocado and Liberty. You can buy his smallest single-origin bars, which I find brilliant for a mid-morning pick-me-up, at Caffè Nero coffee shops.

Mike and James hope that **Chocolarder's** combined factory, museum and cafe in Porthleven will offer the opportunity they crave to introduce a much wider audience to their chocolatey world. I'm longing to visit and will be checking their website (**chocolarder.com**) for regular updates on construction.

Meanwhile, I shall content myself with regular purchases of their outstanding bars. You can buy from the website, from local retailers in Cornwall, from Sourced Market branches and Harrods in London – and from Farmshop at Gloucester services northbound and southbound on the M5, which, if you haven't been there, is far and away the UK's most marvellous motorway service station, and a top-notch chocolate store into the bargain.

THE WONDER OF WILLIE'S

The south west is where the first English-made chocolate bar originated – an item first manufactured by J S Fry and Sons of Bristol in 1847. Fry's – founded, like Cadbury's, by a Quaker family – would eventually be swallowed up by the Birmingham firm and the original Fry's factory at Somerdale in Bristol was an important working part of the Cadbury's empire until the ghastly Kraft takeover almost a decade ago.

During the takeover battle the American firm, told of its history, promised to keep the Bristol factory open. When they won control, they closed it, moving production to Poland and leaving a metaphorical nasty taste in the mouth almost as unpleasant as the actual after-effects of a bar of Dairy Milk.

But the spirit of independent chocolate manufacture in the southwest of England survives, and one spectacular chocolate factory, housed in a series of sheds outside the village of Uffculme in Devon, has earned the kind of virtuous fame that will forever be denied to the faceless twerps of Kraft/Mondelez and their ilk.

Despite a certain amount of televisual notoriety, like all the best chocolate-making locations Willie's chocolate factory is not terribly easy to find. Or perhaps my car's satnav is disabled in some mysterious but powerful way by the aroma of cocoa processing. I punched in the postcode for Willie's HQ, and after a scenic tour of the Wellington area the nice lady announced that "you have arrived at your destination". I begged to differ. No industrial buildings were visible. Come to that, no buildings of any kind were visible. The car had come to a halt at a crossroads with high hedges on three sides and a gate into a field on the fourth. Beyond the gate, a Friesian cow regarded the car with magnificent indifference.

The crossroads boasted an old-fashioned signpost, with destinations still legible on mottled wrought-iron arms. 'Uffculme 2 miles' was one. My father brought me up to try to be early for all meetings, so I was not quite late – yet. And in the village of Uffculme the triumph of technology was thankfully not quite complete. There was a sub-post office staffed by a human being, who knew where Willie's factory was. In fact, I was told, "Everybody knows where Willie's is."

Tell that to the lady in the dashboard, I thought, zooming off with fresh instructions – to arrive on time to the minute. Dad would have been pleased.

"What do you want to do?" said Willie. He was wearing jeans and a leather jacket and bore a striking resemblance to Matt Smith as Doctor Who, only the Doctor tended not to sport a blue hairnet such as Willie modelled right now, in the sort-of reception area of his factory, where he had one hand on a folding wooden table of some age and heft, which he was clearly about to take somewhere if only he could remember where.

"How long have you got? What am I doing next? Are you warm enough?"

The last two questions were directed at a young lady who had appeared from somewhere holding a mobile phone. "Facebook," she said. "In seven minutes. And yes, thank you."

Willie appeared to come to some kind of decision regarding the folding table, and wheeled it into a side office.

"Why don't we walk around a bit and then if I break into Facebook all of a sudden, you won't mind?" He was talking to me again. "Great. Will you stay for lunch? I've got chicken with chocolate mole and rice, it's enough for one but I'm sure I can stretch it to…" he looked at both of us "… three."

"Don't let's worry about that," I said. "Don't worry about anything. Just show me what goes on around here, and let me know if I'm in the way."

"Great," said Willie, and charged off out of the building with me and the young lady with the phone in hot pursuit. "We'll go and look at the bean store. What about Venezuela, eh? It's awful, isn't it? It's amazing how the people there are managing to carry on…"

> " Willie Harcourt-Cooze is a force of nature, and he practically invented bean-to-bar chocolate making in Britain

Willie Harcourt-Cooze is a force of nature, and he practically invented bean-to-bar chocolate making in Britain. Certainly he was responsible for bringing the notion of the ethical, independent chocolate maker to the attention of the public, when in 2008 he made a documentary series with Channel 4 called *Willie's Wonky Chocolate Factory*.

Back then he was running the factory – which occupied a space about the size of a squash court – pretty much single-handedly, and had to improvise an internal Perspex window so he could watch his beloved but fairly ancient machines trundling away in the 'clean space' while catching up on admin in the office.

"Everything was second-hand, or ancient, or both," he recalled. "And most of it is still here, and still in use. See those doors?" He waved towards the kitchen where he experiments with small batches of new beans. "Came from a church. Solid."

Willie had no idea, to begin with, whether he could trust his most magnificent device – a quadruple longitudinal conch which resembles a kind of ancient beam engine, all valves and cylinders and actuating arms – to run overnight. He discovered that he could when, after a particularly exhausting day, he fell asleep on the factory floor and woke the next morning to find the machine still clonking away beside him.

It is tempting to say that Willie's most abiding love is for his machinery. Except that, like Duffy Sheardown up in Cleethorpes, he is manifestly in love with every aspect of the business.

As he walked with me over to the bean shed, a smart padlocked barn at the entrance to the industrial estate, he talked of his concern for his friends in Venezuela and the steps they have had to take to protect their families and their livelihoods in the political chaos that continues to envelop the country. "It is amazing what the people there have been able to do to survive, to protect their livelihood and their families. Amazing."

After a brief struggle, he got the padlock off and a great waft of cacao aroma swept over us. "It's beautiful, isn't it?" Willie said. "But look at this…" and he was off, verbally cataloguing the pile of extraordinary machinery arranged, and in some cases stacked, in a wrapped and orderly manner, to one side of the shed.

There was a tempering machine, a giant shallow cylinder six feet across, and I was sure that I have seen its like somewhere before. "There's one just like that…" I started to say…

"At Cadbury World," Willie breaks in. "Absolutely right. And isn't that pretty much the only bit of kit that they have there? Isn't that awful? I'd love to do a proper chocolate museum one day, these machines are so marvellous. See that, over there in the corner? That came from the Terry's factory in York. Amazing. But, oh yes, we were going to look at the bean store. This way!"

He was off again, opening another, interior door, and suddenly we were surrounded by rows of plump sacks, stacked head-high and each with an evocative name stamped on it: Rio Caribe, Madagascar…

"There's about 70 tons or so in here," Willie said, ticking off the latest arrivals on his fingers. "What shall we try?" He stuck a long, slender metal sampling spoon into a keyhole in a sack and brought out a handful of beans. He crunched one between his fingers and dropped the shards, nib and shell, into the palm of my hand.

I have often tasted cacao nibs before – these days they are almost commonplace as decoration on single-origin bars – but it is always a thrill to get them fresh from the bean. There is a rush of flavour and aroma.

"Gorgeous, aren't they?" Willie said, chomping away. "Try these…" he wheeled around to another sack… "and these…"

We moved on to the production area, pausing so that I could fill in the health and safety questionnaire and don the requisite footwear and hairnet. For all its slightly haphazard appearance and rustic location, Willie's factory is a sophisticated and highly efficient set-up. The charm and energy did not distract from the fact that everything here is done as it should be.

Across the shed from the longitudinal concher – a vision of mock-Edwardian engineering elegance – was a very much more modern piece of kit, a vast and shiny 'one-shot' device, which for those of you unversed in chocolate technology, sploshes precisely the right amount of tempered chocolate to make a bar into the

mould for said bar – except that this machine does several sploshes at once into multiple moulds passing through it on a conveyor belt.

The filled moulds emerge at the other end of the one-shot machine and trundle into another amazing piece of kit, a spiral cooler. More explanation? Willie gave a rapid-fire commentary which I believe I can summarise thus: it's a fridge, but in order to save oneself from having to spend all of one's time taking filled moulds in and out and looking at one's watch, they pop in on a conveyor belt that goes around and around and up and eventually down and the journey takes the amount of time that they would have had to have spent in a fridge if one had simply been popping them in and out by hand.

"Clear? Jolly good. Now, the next bit is quality control…"

After that we joined a group of Willie's team gathered conversationally around a wonderfully Heath-Robinsonesque machine that was somehow wrapping a stack of bars at a time prior to their arrangement in cardboard boxes for distribution to… "All over the country really, which is great. Waitrose! Absolutely. I'm so pleased that we're still with Waitrose."

How much chocolate, I mean, what quantity… what's the simplest way of putting it? How many bars do you make in here, Willie?

He called out a series of number-related enquiries to a lady with a calculator who was monitoring machine print-outs nearby. After some back-and-forth mathematics, he had a rough estimate. "About 30,000 bars a day." Good grief.

"Now, come this way. Let's have a look at the cocoa butter." It was stacked up in boxes in a chilled storeroom. "Tons of it," Willie declared, "and it's beautiful. Do you know the simple test for a good chocolate bar? Look at the label. If it's got vanilla and soya lecithin on it, that's likely to be a rubbish, mass-produced bar."

Why?

<blockquote>
" Willie's enthusiasm is dangerously infectious and it is easy to see how one could be swallowed up fairly rapidly into his organisation
</blockquote>

"People use vanilla – or vanilla flavouring – to cover up the fact that they aren't using great beans. And they use soya lecithin because it makes their ingredients go a lot further. They'll say it makes things consistent, but I can tell you that if they use 1% soya lecithin they save an absolute fortune. I can taste it, though. Nasty. So that's why we use cocoa butter. Lots of it."

After the cocoa butter store, Willie headed back towards the longitudinal conch for his date with Facebook. En route, he explained why the discovery of oil in Venezuela – the kind that makes petroleum – accidentally contributed vastly to the health of the current bean-to-bar chocolate industry.

"Almost everyone in Venezuela stopped growing cacao," he explained. "Why would you, when you could pump oil instead?" So all the old plantations survived, overgrown and neglected – but not ploughed up and replaced by other crops or ruined by deforestation as they were in so many other countries.

When, a few years back, people came looking to revive the cultivation of cacao, they were dismissed as loonies by the oil barons, but they found trees that

preserved many of the oldest and most delicious strains of cacao, and that provided breeding stock for plantations elsewhere in Central America.

"Great, isn't it?" Willie enthused. "Now chocolate is helping to prop up the Venezuelan economy."

Willie's enthusiasm is dangerously infectious, and it is easy to see how one could be swallowed up fairly rapidly into his organisation, joining the happy ranks who answer his constant stream of questions.

"Hettie!" he called out. "Where am I tomorrow? Japan? Peru?"

"Nottingham, Willie."

"Magda! What's 850 times 75? As a percentage?"

"Er…"

"William! What are you making there?"

"Orange."

"Orange. Great! It's organic. It's all organic. William is my son, did I mention that? When am I on Facebook?"

"Now, Willie."

"Really? Are you filming? Right! Have a look at this, chocolate lovers…" And throwing back a lid, he revealed a glossy pool of sloshing chocolate.

There was so much more – more information, more opinions, warm appreciation of fellow chocolate makers – and several more sheds of amazing machinery.

"Willie," I asked at one point, "how many sheds have you actually got here?"

"Um. I'm really not sure."

Eventually we wound up in the warehouse close to where I had come in, where Willie pressed on me many of his most recent innovations – bars, caramels, tablets of cooking chocolate, a jar of chocolate stock ("Brilliant with chicken – get a ton of passata, slosh in the chocolate stock, reduce and serve… here, have another") while a young lady alternately helped him find things and noted down what I was being given.

"Are you sure you won't stay for lunch? Not just a bit? Let me give you another bar or two… What else can I show you?"

I could still be there now, or accompanying Willie on a fact-finding trip to Ecuador, or a diplomatic mission to Malaysia, or anywhere, really, swept up by his relentless charm and energy. But I had to get to Cornwall, so I headed back to the car, staggering under the weight of free goodies and with Willie's warm wishes ringing in my ears.

Now… Cornwall. The satnav messed this one up as well, but there was a pretty good excuse, because the road to Chocolarder's tiny factory is one of ever-decreasing accessibility.

After extricating myself from Willie's remarkable hospitality I trundled onto the M5, which becomes the A30 into Cornwall, and then on a hilltop outside Truro, surrounded by giant windmills, the motorway-like dual carriageway becomes a single lane. The other side of Truro, I turned down a single-track road that I was fairly sure was Frog Hill, and there the satnav announced our arrival with the familiar misplaced confidence.

Several U-turns later I turned, more in hope than expectation, down a lumpy track deep in a wooded valley. At the foot of the track a giant viaduct on tall brick arches loomed above, and in the shadow of the arches, like broken teeth, stood the stumps of a previous viaduct long broken and disused.

I pulled into a yard fringed with vaguely maritime hulks and long-defunct vans. In the background a river babbled powerfully and somewhere a dog barked.

"Andrew!" I jumped about a yard in the air, and when I returned to earth a tall and bearded figure was offering a confident handshake. "You found us! Well done!"

This was Mike Longman of Chocolarder, a former chef and patissier who makes bean-to-bar creations of quite remarkable beauty and sophistication… here.

The Viaduct Works at Frog Hill has one or two similarities with Willie's set-up in Devon – shed, industrial estate – but Chocolarder's premises are much more rudimentary. Not unlike Willie's must have been when he was starting out.

Where the double-barrelled Devonian has tens of tons of beans stacked up in his storehouse – enough to last a smaller operation for years – Mike has perhaps a couple of dozen stacks in two storage areas. Of necessity, he sources beans in a more modest way than Willie, and his links with those who grow the beans are still developing – a process that he longs to speed up and improve.

When he worked as a chef, most notably at an acclaimed restaurant called the Hop Kitchen, he recalled that he and his colleagues in the kitchen were close to their suppliers in every sense.

> **We get people – well-meaning people – who show up on the doorstep and say, 'We bought some of your chocolate and we saw the address on the back. We're in Cornwall on holiday and thought we'd love to see what a real chocolate factory is like.' And in they come…**

"We knew the fishermen who caught the fish," he said, "the farmers who raised the cattle for the beef and grew the wheat that made our bread. That kind of direct contact with where the food came from was a huge part of being a chef for me."

When the raw material is chocolate, geography and climate dictate that the process is more distant. "No matter where the beans are grown, the farmers are growing for an industry that they barely know, whose needs they often don't understand," Mike explained. "They are so far away, so detached from the people who are going to use the beans, who are going to taste the chocolate."

So an important, and gentle, and mutually educational process has to take place whereby the farmers teach the chocolate makers about how and where the beans are grown, about which elements of the landscape, neighbouring vegetation and climate may affect the flavour of the beans, about how they are harvested and stored, and the makers try to let the cacao growers know about how the beans are used in the factory, about what flavour profiles they are trying to achieve, and about how things such as harvest techniques, fermentation and storage before transport can affect quality and taste.

This is the kind of delicate diplomatic process that Willie has conducted over many years, with the additional advantage that Willie's Cacao is now dealing in quantities of beans that give him a lot of influence over farming and storage practices on the ground.

It is a long way from the factory under the viaduct on Frog Hill to the Dominican Republic or Madagascar. Come to think of it, it is a long way from Frog Hill to almost anywhere. But Mike knows that constant communication with growers has to be the way forward, just as he knows that bringing the people who buy his chocolate closer to how it is made will ensure loyalty and engagement.

"Our new building in Porthleven will make all that happen," Mike promised, casting an eye around his current, less-than-palatial surroundings. Right now, visitors can be more of an inconvenience than a boon.

"We get people – well-meaning people – who show up on the doorstep and say, 'We bought some of your chocolate and we saw the address on the back. We're in Cornwall on holiday and thought we'd love to see what a real chocolate factory is like.' And in they come…"

What a real chocolate factory is like – in this case – is busy, and small, and rather cluttered, but also clean and hygienic, and not at all geared up to accommodating and educating visitors.

The new set-up, currently under construction, will aim to do all of those things, while also providing a scaled-up production facility for Mike and his colleague James, who is scheduled to do the bulk of the making while Mike concentrates on innovation and experimentation.

"We're going to have a cafe, a museum and factory behind glass," Mike declared. A set-up, it appears, not unlike that realised by Sophie Jewett at York Cocoa House.

"The idea is that we will no longer be making things in isolation," Mike said. "Right now we make bars and chocolates and send them out and just hope that people get it. When we move we'll be able to bring people in and show them how we do it."

That will solve the problem of 'walk-in' visitors and also allow Mike and James to retire some of their more ancient and improvised pieces of kit, such as the bean roaster adapted from a baker's oven that might have been expected to see out its days gently raising cakes, the winnower that is essentially a sausage stuffer with an Archimedean screw, and the 45kg conching drums.

Mike described these as 'bog-standard', but they have in fact been modified in a typically Cornish way. "They needed new engines and gearboxes," Mike said, "so obviously we asked the boat builders across the way to have a look." And the boat builders, unsurprisingly, recommended second-hand boat engines and gearboxes that they just happened to have lying around. "Worked a treat," Mike said. "We've had them four years and I should think they have worked three years non-stop in that time."

The most treasured industrial item, though, is one that would turn Willie Harcourt-Cooze green with envy, as Mike delightedly noted.

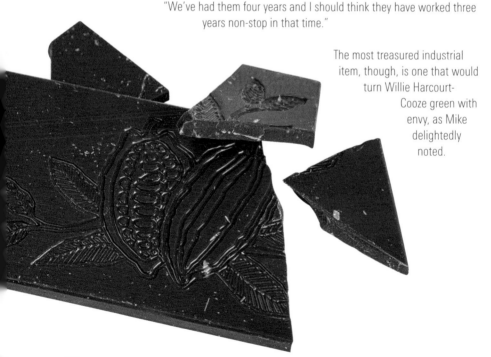

Chocolarder's bean cracker is a marzipan-making machine manufactured, according to the brass plate on the cherrywood hopper, in Maastricht in the Netherlands in the 1920s. This gorgeous mechanical marvel, a gently clonking vision of cogs and rollers, is powered by an engine that is even older, and celebrated its centenary last year. It is running, Mike calculates, at around 10% of its intended power – but that turns out to be an ideal output for the gentle separation of cocoa-bean husks from nibs.

"The truth is that I want all of my machines to be like that, to be beautiful," Mike mused, and I told him that he sounded uncannily like Willie enthusing over one of his latest acquisitions, a giant and ancient cocoa-butter press that I had been privileged to encounter just hours earlier.

> " Chocolarder's bean cracker is a marzipan-making machine manufactured, according to the brass plate on the cherrywood hopper, in Maastricht in the Netherlands in the 1920s

"Oh heavens, he's got one, has he? I long to get hold of one of those," Mike said. "Tell me, can you remember exactly where it was at Willie's place? And do you know if he happens to lock that shed up at night?"

I said that, regrettably for Mike's nefarious purposes, I was pretty sure that Willie's security was as tight as a drum, and Mike sighed and took me into his kitchen to taste one or two of his latest concoctions.

One of the things that I have noticed on my travels is that, while all chocolate makers have one substance in common, their approaches to it, and the ways in which their plans develop, all differ. Their passions intersect here and there, like chocolately Venn diagrams, but each has an individual vision.

Mike Longman makes bean-to-bar chocolate, like Duffy Sheardown, and is branching out into caramels, like Willie Harcourt-Cooze. He plans to build a working factory open to the public, like Sophie Jewett and, like Paul A Young, he is fascinated by the wilder fringes of chocolate flavours and the possibility of exotic combinations.

He shares with Young a background as a top-class chef-patissier, and that influences his thinking about future directions.

Have I found, Mike wanted to know, anyone in the UK making bean-to-bar chocolate who is also making a lot of filled chocolates?

I'm not sure that I have. Chococo make a few bars, but not from beans, and Willie makes his lovely caramels...

"It's strange, isn't it?" Mike pronounced. "But that's the kind of thing I really want to do."

Mike is an economics graduate, as well as a chef, and a remarkable communicator. He speaks fairly rapidly but what he says is well thought out and his arguments are sound and convincing. He runs with ideas that occur to him but never forgets what he is trying to say, and the stream of information and theory was so interesting that I rarely interrupted and just let him get on with it, while I nibbled at fragments of a dark bar with oats that he had offered me. I nibbled subtly, so as not to distract him.

"There is so much that can be done now to push the boundaries of what chocolate can be," Mike said. "So much more that can be done with techniques that we have now. Look, hang on..." He reached up to a shelf in the kitchen and brought down an airtight box. "Have some of this."

The box was filled with chunks of what looked like halva, or a similar Arabic nut-based confection.

"Try it", Mike suggested, and I popped a piece into my mouth, where it instantly melted, releasing a cascade of salty sweetness. "It's a pavé, made with green olives," he explained.

Of course it was... "And I'm going to use it with this," he waved a jar, "which is local tree honey, so deep and rich, and with peanut mousse. And all of that can be enrobed in beautiful bean-to-bar chocolate."

Good grief, I wanted to exclaim, in the manner of Dr Watson praising a revelation by Sherlock Holmes, this is the stuff of genius. Instead I just said that it sounds wonderful, which is perfectly true.

"I'm so glad that you like it, that you can see where I'm going," Mike said.

One of the great pleasures of chocolate is that there is such a wide range of origins and strengths and… manifestations of the substance available to those who want to play with it, from the powerful 100% dark, such as those that Willie Harcourt-Cooze is employing in his new sugar-free fruit and nut bars, to the mildest of white chocolates that are almost all meltingly delicate cocoa butter.

And not only is the range of chocolate so vast, but the range of responses to it is almost infinite. "It is such a subjective thing to eat," Mike declared. "The fulfilment – and the frustration – is pretty much continuous."

I suspect that, like Willie up the M5 in Devon, it is the limitless complexity of raw material and process that Mike finds so endlessly fascinating, and he confirmed as much. Making chocolate, he explained, is an unimprovable combination of science and art.

"You have chemistry and physics in the processes," he said. "The pressures that you need to crack and crush, the temperatures that you need for melting. The physics of conching a bean to fragments 25 microns across so that they can be efficiently enrobed in cocoa butter, then the chemistry again of tempering that. And then you have to bring the outcome of all of those processes together in a bar, in something that will provide people with a sensory experience."

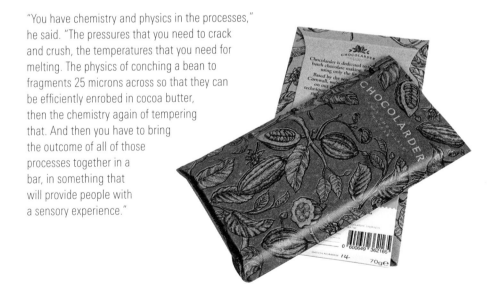

He laughed. "You know, I only got into this because I was just a pastry chef who wanted to see more of his kids"

Those children, Amelie and Sullivan, aged five and two, are – to their father's genial puzzlement – not all that keen on chocolate. Yet. But they will no doubt be thrilled to reveal to future classmates what their father does for a living.

Older local residents are more supportive. Indeed, most of Chocolarder's thriving business has been built locally, by word of mouth and with the understanding of sensible shopkeepers.

"That has been a huge bonus, and I think it is a benefit of being away from the big cities." Mike found when he was starting out that he could walk into a shop in Truro or one of the surrounding towns and villages and explain to the owner what he was doing – and be received without derision or apathy.

Instead, when he offered a shopkeeper a taste of one of his bars – the now-celebrated dark milk with gorse flower, say – they would give it a try. And then confess that they had never tasted anything like it.

"It's fair to say that a good few people were blown away," Mike admitted, almost sheepishly.

So when they then asked him how much he was asking for a bar and he replied, well, £5, they didn't laugh in his face but instead said: "OK – we'll sell it."

The business grew rapidly, to a point where Chocolarder had a remarkable customer profile: 90% of sales were local, and all the rest were from the Farmshop at Gloucestershire services on the M5 – and from Harrods Food Hall.

"People down here, they know what they're buying," Mike said. "They're loyal, and they like to share." Any chocolate maker's dream customer profile.

☐ The bars are the thing for me: I love Willie's trademark square shapes and his classic flavours. The Sambirano Gold 71% dark from Madagascar (a steal, like all these bars, at £2.99) is one of my all-time favourites – lovely red-fruit flavour notes that are utterly characteristic of Madagascar's cacao, and a beautiful snap and texture. Another that I love is equally distinctive: the Surabaya Gold 69% dark from Indonesia has the smoky note that is typical of the region and comes from the fermentation methods used only there.

TASTING NOTES

☐ The Willie's Cacao range is large and growing all the time: the latest additions are powerful, entirely sugar-free bars made with 100% chocolate and fruit and nut inclusions. I enjoy them very much but they are not for the timid.

☐ Willie's Black Pearls are brilliantly moreish caramels in dark chocolate which are terrific for passing around with coffee after dinner (or demolishing at work, if you are less refined). They come in three different varieties, at £6.59 a box on Willie's website. His truffles are ace too.

☐ One of the easiest, cheapest and tastiest ways to introduce yourself, or a fortunate friend, to the range of distinctive flavours that single-origin bean-to-bar chocolate can provide is to get hold of the box of Willie's bars called Wonders of the World, which for £10.99 brings you five bars from widely different growing regions. Compare, contrast – and enjoy.

☐ Which of the Chocolarder bars to choose (there are many)? Mike Longman may not thank me for saying this, since it has become the chocolate equivalent of a greatest hit that a musician is always required to play, but the wild gorse flower dark milk, made with 50% Nicaraguan Chuno cacao and gorse flowers harvested by Mike from the hedgerows of Cornish coastal paths, is one of the most delicately delicious bars of chocolate that you will ever come across, and is rapidly becoming a global legend among chocolate makers. You really must try it.

☐ All of Chocolarder's bars are £4.99 – great value, given the work that goes into them – and, like Willie, they offer an excellent tasting box: the Complete Craft selection at £45 for nine terrific bars. The sea salt caramel truffles, £14 a box, are dreamy.

☐ Also try Chocolarder's Ashaninka 72% dark from Peru, made from the same beans used raw by Forever Cacao in Wales – an excellent opportunity to assess which treatment of the same bean works best. Their Ottange Farm 74% from Madagascar is a wonderful example of the fruity flavours that typify that amazing island's cacao.

LONDON

CAPITAL APPRECIATION

USEFUL INFO

Paul A Young

paulayoung.co.uk

At his three pretty shops Paul has a huge range of his own filled chocolates, bars and novelties, as well as a few first-rate artisanal bars, notably the full range from Duffy Sheardown.

143 Wardour Street, Soho, London W1F 8WA

Open: Mon–Sat 10am–8pm; Sun and bank hols noon–7pm

By Tube: Tottenham Court Road station is a 10-minute walk

33 Camden Passage, Islington, London N1 8EA

Open: Mon–Thu 10am–6.30pm; Fri 10am–7pm; Sat 10am–6.30pm; Sun 11am–6pm

By Tube: Angel station is a 5-minute walk

20 The Royal Exchange, Threadneedle Street, London EC3V 3LP

Open: Mon–Fri 9am–7pm.

By Tube: Bank station is a 5-minute walk

Selfridges

400 Oxford Street, London W1A 1AB

Open: Mon–Sat 9.30am–9pm; Sun 11.30am–6pm

By Tube: Bond Street station is a 5-minute walk

Harrods

87–135 Brompton Road, London SW1X 7XL

Open: Mon–Sat 10am–9pm; Sun 11.30am–6pm

By Tube: Knightsbridge station is a 5-minute walk

Rococo Chocolates

Chantal Coady has been making beautiful chocolates in London for donkey's years. Lovely soft centres and caramels, a huge range of flavoured bars, and also bean-to-bar treats from the Grenada Chocolate Company, an excellent Caribbean set-up.

Branches in Marylebone, Chelsea, Belgravia, Notting Hill and Covent Garden; for address details and opening times, go to **rococochocolates.com/locations**

Sourced Market has a good range of bars from a variety of artisan makers, including Land of Bethnal Green in East London and other UK makers.

Branches at St Pancras Station; in Clerkenwell, Victoria and Marylebone; for address details and opening times, go to **sourcedmarket.com**

Watch out for the pop-up events at the covered market in King's Cross hosted by **Cocoa Runners** – these boast a great turn-out of chocolate makers from all over the UK and further afield and are a great chance to meet and talk with some of the biggest names in artisanal chocolate. Keep an eye on **cocoarunners.com** for details of pop-up markets, as well as maker-guided tastings.

The Chocolate Museum

187 Ferndale Road, London SW9 8BA

By car: Unlike in central London, there is a reasonable chance of parking nearby, especially at weekends.

By Tube: Brixton station is a 10-minute walk

Open: Wed–Fri 2–7pm; Sat–Sun 11am–6pm

Informative and charming small-scale museum; the shop stocks a few good-quality bars, including Duffy's and Lucocoa.

Prestat

14 Princes Arcade, St James's, London SW1Y 6DS

By Tube: Piccadilly Circus station is a 5-minute walk

Open: Mon–Fri 9.30am–6pm, Sat 10am–5pm; Sun 11am–4.30pm

Stylish filled chocolates (I recommend the red velvet truffles; my mother recommends the gin truffles) in a lovely, tiny technicolour shop/cafe in one of London's most characterful arcades.

Pierre Marcolini

37 Marylebone High Street, London W1U 4QE

By Tube: Baker Street and Bond Street stations are both about a 10-minute walk

Open: Mon–Sat 10am–6.30pm; Sun 10.30am–6.30pm

Pierre is a Belgian and does not make chocolate in the UK, but he does make lovely shiny chocolately things and one must be cosmopolitan once in a while.

I must also say that after extensive research I have concluded that his hot chocolate, with whipped chocolate cream and chocolate meringues on top, is the best such concoction to be found in the capital, and even at £5 a cup is well-nigh irresistible.

Artisan du Chocolat

Justly famous salted caramel truffles, and a huge range of bars made in Kent but sold in A du C's shops in Chelsea, Kensington, West Hampstead, in Selfridges and at a regular stall in Borough Market; for store details see **artisanduchocolat.com**. Full disclosure: my face is on the wrapper of one of their bars; don't hold this against them.

WHERE IT ALL BEGAN

The first recorded chocolate shop in London, it is generally agreed, was opened by a Frenchman in 1657 in Queen's Head Alley, not far from what is now Liverpool Street station in the City, the financial district of the metropolis.

I thought it would be fun, or at least instructive, to go and see what stood on the spot now, but quickly discovered that Queen's Head Alley had long ago ceased to exist, what with the Great Fire and the Blitz and the endless march of speculative development.

According to the history.ac.uk website, the Alley was now mostly beneath Union Court, south of Wormwood Street and west of Bishopsgate Street.

So one lunchtime I left my desk in Victoria and hopped on the Tube to Liverpool Street, emerging 20 minutes later among sweaty hordes of City workers scampering around in search of their lunchtime victuals.

I crossed Wormwood Street — which sounds like it should branch off Diagon Alley in Hogsmeade, but is in fact a dual carriageway lined with bookies and barbers — and walked south on Old Broad Street, looking for Union Court.

There was no sign of it. Built over, by yet another colossal bank. I paused for a moment on a nameless ramp in almost the right spot, noting down the old blue plaque recording the site of the house of the fabulously wealthy City merchant Thomas Gresham. No sooner had I halted than a smart security guard advanced upon me, wanting to know my business.

"Union Court? Never heard of it. But you can't stand here…"

Ten yards further south was another nameless alley, in the shadow of Tower 42, formerly known as the NatWest Tower and still one of the City's tallest skyscrapers. The little paved pedestrian route was the closest I would get to Queen's Head Alley, and on its corner with Old Broad Street stood a French bakery, a branch of the upmarket patisserie chain Paul.

It suddenly occurred to me that a historical circle could be closed here, so I marched inside and asked the young – and, it turned out, French – man behind the counter if I might have a hot chocolate.

"Mais bien sur," he said, and swiftly produced a steaming cardboard cup.

I took Paul's Signature Hot Chocolate to a seat in the window. It was good: rich and thick as an Old Harrovian moneybroker, and identifiably containing real chocolate. As I sipped, I watched the squadrons of financiers, drones and PAs march past, squawking into phones or prodding at their screens, clutching cups and paper bags from Pret and Paul.

Their concerns and conversations were unlikely to have been very different from those who walked past the earliest chocolate shop on this site, and while the skyline had changed, the essential topography had not. To my right I could see Wormwood Street become London Wall, its route established by the Romans; to my left Old Broad Street followed its pre-Fire route, curving downhill towards the Thames.

My cup of chocolate was probably somewhat different from that served by the anonymous Frenchman, however. The chocolate served to London's earliest consumers, and enjoyed by keen trenchermen such as Samuel Pepys, who employed it as a hangover cure, was made with hot water rather than milk, and flavoured with spices.

Chocolate first arrived in Europe with conquistadors returning to Spain from Central America, and was only later adapted to pander to local tastes.

The gifted Soho chocolatier Paul A Young is an expert on early chocolate recipes, and if you wish to replicate the drink as enjoyed in Queen's Head Alley then his recipe for 'Aztec-style' hot chocolate is the way to go:

25g light muscovado sugar
    (more if you like it sweet)
20g dark cocoa powder
100g Caribbean 66% dark chocolate
Spice of your choice, e.g. chilli,
    cinnamon, nutmeg, cardamom
    or ginger

DIRECTIONS

☐ Heat 500 millilitres of water, the sugar and cocoa powder in a pan and simmer for three minutes. Break the chocolate into pieces and add to the pan.

☐ Using an electric hand mixer, blend for one minute, adding any spices that you are using at this point. Bring the hot chocolate back to simmer for two minutes and serve.

Further exploration of the culinary possibilities of chocolate – and respect for the people who grow it – can be enjoyed south of the river at Borough Market. There was a thriving market here in medieval times, long before chocolate first came ashore in England, and the location remains a magnet for foodies from all over the UK – and throngs of visiting tourists.

A good number of stallholders offer filled chocolates and artisan bars – indeed, Artisan du Chocolat, whose sugar-free bar is graced by my own photograph on its wrapper, is often to be found here – but the cast frequently changes so it is as well to dive in and enjoy what you find. But a permanent fixture overlooking the indoor section of the market is Rabot 1745, the restaurant offshoot of Hotel Chocolat, named after the company estate in St Lucia and the date of its founding.

Here you can sit on a terrace overlooking the bustling market and enjoy Caribbean cocktails and dishes created at Boucan, the restaurant at the company's luxury hotel in St Lucia – the actual Hotel Chocolat. It's a terrific and unusual spot for a foodie outing.

Back across the river, where best to find unusual and artisan chocolate?

There are certain establishments that are synonymous with the concept of shopping in London: for example, Harrods, Selfridges and Fortnum & Mason. Their fame is a guarantor of congestion rather than quality, but each of the trio will reward a visit by the determined chocolate hunter who is not easily distracted.

> **The Single Estate chocolate bar is a recent innovation which aims to apply something of the cachet of fine wines to fine chocolate**

Harrods is the geographical outlier of the three, dominating Knightsbridge like a stately ocean liner surrounded by flashy little speedboats. The exterior is little changed from its Edwardian heyday, but the innards have undergone a series of tacky makeovers at the hands of Egyptian and Qatari owners that have left swathes of the store looking like a low-ceilinged pharaonic Disneyland.

Forge on through the confused crowds to the Food Hall, though, and shreds of previous dignity are preserved, surrounding an excellent selection of chocs.

The Art Nouveau tiling on the walls is splendid, and there are concessions for a quality crowd of chocolatiers including old-school stalwarts such as Charbonnel et Walker and Godiva – but there is also a surprisingly tasteful range of bars. I was delighted to find bars from the excellent and lovely Amelia Rope, a London maker, and Chocolarder's range from distant Cornwall being examined by cosmopolitan shoppers, and also surprised by Harrods' own-brand single-estate bars.

The single-estate chocolate bar is a recent innovation which aims to apply something of the cachet of fine wines to fine chocolate. The idea is that beans harvested from a specific location will possess unique characteristics beyond those conferred by nationality or cacao variety.

Not only has Harrods explored this retail niche, usually the preserve of small and specialised producers, but it has sought out some particularly obscure origins, and offers the results at decidedly keen prices.

So not far from £10,000 handbags, the chocolate fan can locate a bar of 76% dark chocolate from the Old Plantation at Malekula Island in Vanuatu – that is bean-to-bar chocolate which I can assure you is not available anywhere else in the UK. What is even more astonishing in this location is that the wide range of single-origin bars is fairly keenly priced, at £6 for each 70g bar.

It would be lovely to report that somewhere in the million-square-feet Harrods building is a dedicated artisan grinding and tempering to make the bars from scratch – but that is not the case. The bars are made 'exclusively for Harrods', and the wrappers don't say by whom… but I would hazard a guess that they are made in the shadow of Wormwood Scrubs by a first-class – and rather shy – company that makes own-brand chocolates for many of Britain's retail heavyweights.

It could be that you feel that £6 is too modest a price for a souvenir chocolate bar from Harrods, in which case I direct you to the bars they stock from To'ak, by some distance the most expensive chocolate bars on general sale anywhere in the world.

To'ak bars are not only from very specific locations in Central America, but are also of a certain 'vintage', having been matured in casks imbued with the flavour of quality spirits. The resulting bars are then packaged in little caskets made from rather beautiful wood, and sold with a great deal of hoopla and paraphernalia for… £375 for 50g.

Yes I have tasted them, and no, they aren't worth it.

If you still have any money left, head for the West End and have a look at Selfridges, Fortnum's and a smart little shop with more charm than either.

Selfridges had a brief flirtation with the idea of becoming a one-stop shop for bean-to-bar aficionados, and for a few months a couple of years ago their Chocolate Wall, with resident expert curator, was a thing of wonder and beauty. But it didn't last, and the Wall came down, to be replaced by a less inspiring range of own-brand bars.

Selfridges has undergone a top-to-toe revamp even more extensive than that at Harrods, and has emerged shiny and overlit and bearing a powerful resemblance, in décor, ambience and clientele, to the duty-free mall at Dubai International Airport.

At least there remains a sizeable chocolate zone, though with the standard duty-free concentration on shiny and somewhat bland international brands. So, once you have negotiated the scent stands and the beauty counters with a handkerchief clamped over your nostrils, this is a good spot to tuck into strawberries dipped in molten Godiva chocolate (don't be taken in by the Belgian heritage and hoopla – it's owned by Turks), and an even better spot to score a £60 box from the same maker's 'Royal Suede' range, aimed at the kind of customer who thinks that something called Royal that comes in a suede wrapper simply has to be classy.

There are outposts of goodness in concessions for Artisan du Chocolat and Pierre Marcolini (see Useful Info at the start of this chapter) but in chocolate terms we have to conclude that Selfridges' best years are behind them.

One stop south on the Jubilee Line (or 10 minutes down Park Lane in your chauffeur-driven limo, turning left at Hyde Park Corner), Fortnum's has evolved from slightly fussy grocer to the Empire into a frantically branded upmarket theme park. The upper floors are for clothes and scent and stuff (why? Who goes to Fortnum's for an overcoat?) and the ground floor is swamped with own-brand biscuits and jams.

For a swift chocolate hit, turn right through the front doors for glass counters crammed with immaculate soft centres and rows of Fortnum's branded bars. These are competently made for F & M elsewhere (most likely in the same spot as Harrods' bars) but rather more desperately packaged with gimmicky names. The sugar-free dark bar, for example, is called Goodnight, My Bittersweet Beloved, and things edge further towards the X-rated with the dark-with-chilli bar called The Beast Comes At Midnight.

Fortnum's has an entire counter dedicated to its version of what it calls 'naturally occurring' ruby chocolate, a pink bar which it would love you to think is made from beans which are naturally pink. In fact, the beans look just like any other beans, and the colour is present only as a precursor, unlocked by an industrial process which took the chocolate manufacturers Barry Callebaut years to invent. Natural… in a sense, then.

There are some good and interesting points about Fortnum's, but they don't have anything to do with chocolate. In fact, they are all out of the way: in the basement deli you can put together a delicious and not madly expensive lunchbox – London's canniest office workers take these back to their desks; on the walls of the smart stair lobbies between floors hangs an excellent collection of 20th-century art comprising one of London's best free galleries; and on the roof there are four little buildings in which workers produce the only foodstuff manufactured from scratch on the premises.

> They are not just any old beehives but six-foot-tall behemoths, twice the size of normal hives and constructed, what is more, in four different architectural styles: Roman, Mughal, Chinese and Gothick

They are beehives – but, this being Fortnum's, they are not just any old beehives but six-foot-tall behemoths, twice the size of normal hives and constructed, what is more, in four different architectural styles: Roman, Mughal, Chinese and Gothick. The hives, which have been established now for more than a decade, are painted in the store's signature eau de Nil shade and the beekeeper, Steven Benbow, harvests a crop of honey every September.

So if you are in the store stocking up on ruby chocolate (which isn't at all bad, actually – pretty, and tasting not unlike a white chocolate flavoured with red berries) be sure to ask if they have some of that year's crop of Fortnum's bees' honey. It will taste, they say, of the flowers wherever the bees have chosen to forage in the previous year, and the closest concentration of flowers is in the garden of Buckingham Palace.

The Big Three are quite diverting in a vast and vulgar way, but a good introduction to London's marvellous little chocolate shops can be had just a few yards away. Turn right out of the front door of Fortnum & Mason and pass a little way along Piccadilly and you will come, on your right, to Prince's Arcade, the most recently refurbished of two such arcades on the south side of Piccadilly.

Here will you find the tiny, bright and very pretty Prestat shop, the only stand-alone store (they have concessions elsewhere) of the chocolate makers by appointment to HM the Queen.

Prestat are not bean-to-bar makers or artisans, but they are immensely accomplished chocolatiers and produce on a scale that allows them to work with originality, versatility and terrific quality control. In their immaculate little factory just around the corner from the North Pole train-cleaning depot in northwest London they make a wide range of filled chocolates, truffles and bars – as well as chocolates and bars that are branded with some of the most celebrated names in British retail.

I have been privileged to enjoy a couple of visits there and the storeroom, crammed with precious spices, preserves and sweet treats from all over the world, is a cornucopia of delight that cannot fail to call to mind the work of Prestat's most famous fan: Roald Dahl, author of *Charlie and the Chocolate Factory* – who made Prestat's truffles central to the plot of his salacious novel *My Uncle Oswald*.

The factory is not open to the public, alas, but the little store is a charming showcase for every single one of their brightly

packaged products, and the smartly turned out and almost excessively polite manager offers well-informed assistance.

I am very fond of Prestat's Pink Everest bar, made with dark chocolate and pink Himalayan salt, and I tasted their red velvet truffles at the prototype stage and have adored them ever since. My mother, she would wish me to record, is a fan of their gin truffles, while my late father was particularly fond of their dark chocolate thins.

If you enjoy people-watching as well as confectionery, order a cup of hot chocolate and perch on one of the stools in Prestat's window to sip and watch the parade of humanity walk past. It may not be a cast that accurately represents the native population of London, but you are guaranteed as great a line-up of the rich and infamous as you will see at Madame Tussaud's... and these are the real thing.

A cup of first-rate hot chocolate is also a must at the branches of Rococo, in Belgravia, Chelsea and on Marylebone High Street. Like Prestat, Rococo is a veteran of the London chocolate scene and there is a connection to the big department stores through its founder and guiding light.

Chantal Coady started out on the confectionery counter in Harrods Food Hall, and dreamed of one day having her own luxury chocolate emporium. She will, if you are lucky, tell you some scurrilous tales about the romantic adventures with dashing and well-connected types that led to her setting up on her own as a chocolatier, but you should be advised that most, if not all of them, are invented to tease those who ask her the hackneyed question: "So, how did you get into chocolate making?"

The truth is that, being a practical young lady, she didn't stand around in Harrods dreaming for long but got on with creating, and Rococo has been a roaring success for more than 35 years, earning Chantal an OBE for services to chocolate and the boundless gratitude of discerning customers.

Rococo combines elegant good taste with imaginative flavours and a vital connection to the people who actually grow the raw materials.

ETHICAL COCOA

Rococo's collaboration with the trail-blazing Grenada Chocolate Company started in 2002. Enchanted by this solar-powered, tree-to-bar company on the spice island of Grenada, Chantal and husband James – Rococo's ...man – started investing in organic cocoa.

474

THE ROCOCO
FAIRY TALE

Once upon a time there was an inquisitive little English girl who dreamed of a world filled with choc...

Inspired by the adventures of ...
Wonka, Chantal opens ...
shop straight out ...
a fresh coa...
scene...

GRENADA

178

It would be relatively easy to fill a book with people who take other people's factory-made chocolate and fill it with fancy ingredients, wrap it in gilded paper and stick on a huge mark-up. But that is not the kind of chocolate that I like. The kind of chocolate that I like is made by good people in the right way, with respect and proper reward for those who grow, harvest and process the raw materials, as well as those who dream up the flavour combinations and design the packaging.

Chantal knows that her customers expect her chocolates to taste delicious and look pretty – an early design partner was Kitty Arden, who is also responsible for the branding of Prestat. But she also believes sincerely in the importance of encouraging young makers – and supporting the communities where cacao is grown.

So alongside the elegant boxes and bars in her shops you will see bars from the Grenada Chocolate Company, not only grown and harvested on the little Caribbean island but made into chocolate there as well in a solar-powered factory that provides jobs and income for the local people. The commercial partnership between Rococo and the GCC is a terrific example of engaged ethics – and terrific bars, because the fresh, crisp Grenadian slabs are among my favourites for sharing.

So London is not short of grand shops that sell chocolate, and it also has smart little chocolate shops. It also has some brave artisan makers who are yet to open their own premises.

The only pioneer in recent history to both make chocolate bars from scratch and sell those bars on the same premises was Dom Ramsey of Damson Chocolate in Chapel Market in Islington.

It's a fantastic line-up, with a spine of classics — a dark Madagascan, a Vietnam Lam Dong, but also imaginative experiments such as Icelandic-style liquorice and sea salt dark milk that any Scandinavian chocolate fan would adore

This was not the chi-chi Islington of old New Labour politicians-turned-PRs in Georgian houses, or internet incubators in converted Victorian schools — Chapel Market is an old-fashioned, mixed-up, fully functioning street market flanked by shops and restaurants of every kind. There are salt-beef bars and bookmakers, knock-off clothes stalls and mobile-phone repair booths.

And at the far end — you could follow the bewitching odour on the breeze, if it was blowing your way — was the little shop/factory of Damson Chocolate.

Dom, the founder and guiding spirit, worked in the office surrounded by sacks — full-size, both-arms-and-all-your-strength-to-shift-them sacks — of cocoa beans.

The back room was a stripped-down, squeaky-clean space where the walls were lined with shiny, stainless machines.

Back out front, at the shop counter, Dom would talk you through the Damson range — a bowl of freshly broken tasting chunks set out before the rows of each individual bar. It was a fantastic line-up, with a spine of classics — a dark Madagascan, a Vietnam Lam Dong, but also imaginative experiments such as Icelandic-style liquorice and sea salt dark milk that any Scandinavian chocolate fan would adore.

A lifelong chocolate lover, he first got involved in the culinary scene with a blog — Chocablog — which has been running for more than a decade and is one of the most authoritative and well informed in what is now a crowded space. He became a judge with the Academy of Chocolate and International Chocolate Awards and was a founding member of the team at Cocoa Runners, the international bean-to-bar supermarket based (and thriving) just up the road from his current premises.

But all along his dream was to make his own bars, and after helping out other makers and picking up skills and tips wherever he could, Dom founded Damson with Tom Millson in 2015. A nasty fire not long after they had established the base in Chapel Market almost put paid to the project, but with support from friends, fellow chocolate fiends and imaginative food entrepreneurs, Dom pushed on.

You might have noticed, though, that I have been using the past tense over the last few paragraphs. I loved to visit Damson, and Dom is unquestionably a hero of the bean-to-bar trade. But just at the moment the little shop on Chapel Market is closed, and we wait to see what the future holds for Damson Chocolate.

What he is trying to do — to make and sell good bean-to-bar chocolate in the same premises in central London — is almost unimaginably difficult, as he himself admits. But the prospect lingers in the mind.

"It's tough," Dom admits, sharing a chunk of his latest, sumptuous coffee-and-cream dark milk bar. "But I wouldn't have it any other way. My shop. My factory. My dream."

Ginger-bearded, twinkly and genial, Paul A Young has become one of Britain's best-known chocolatiers through frequent appearances in print, online and on television, most notably making the treats of yesteryear in the deliciously nostalgic series *The Sweet Makers*.

But there is substance behind the fluency and charm: years of training as a pastry chef, working at an early stage with the superstar chef Marco Pierre White, and years of experience in the kitchens of his shops.

There are branches in Camden and Threadneedle Street in the City, but the most substantial Paul A Young emporium is in Soho. This is a must-visit location not only for fans of filled chocolates – for Young is one of the finest exponents of those in the world – but also for barflys, because he stocks a full range of bars made by the wonderful Cleethorpes bean-to-bar maestro Duffy Sheardown (see my chapter on The East). What is more, Young serves an enormously tempting cup of hot chocolate ladled, in the winter months, from a glorious copper cauldron steaming in the shop window. What better way to lure in customers on a chilly day?

The Barnsley-born Young is often to be found exploring new flavour combinations in the kitchen in the shop's basement. There are frequent chocolate-making classes here as well, and there is no one better at imparting, in a kindly and witty manner, the mysteries of tempering and ganache making.

But he is at his best inventing wonderful new combinations of fine chocolate and delicious fillings, and it would be a foolish visitor to London who departed the capital without sampling at least several of Young's most celebrated truffles – the Marmite version, for example, which I adore, the beer and crisp version made with Camden's BrewDog ale, or the homage to his roots in the Yorkshire tea and biscuit truffle. These and many, many more are laid out in mouthwatering rows in Young's shops, freshly made and so to be consumed as soon as possible. That is not a difficult piece of advice to heed.

As one of the finest shopping cities in the world, London is not short of places to buy chocolate. But as one of the finest shopping cities in the world, it is also not short of places charging rip-off prices for ordinary, dull or mass-produced chocolate. Mainly because of the loopy cost of commercial space in the city, it is all but impossible to combine bean-to-bar chocolate making and a retail space in London – in fact, Dom Ramsey is the only person I know of who has tried it recently. There are one or two other bean-to-bar makers at work in the capital, though, and while their kitchens are not normally open to the public it is certainly more than worthwhile to look out for their bars online or in London's few top-quality chocolate-bar outlets.

One of them is a protégé of Paul A Young. But Phil Landers has gone down the bar rather than filled chocolate route and produces immaculate slabs of single-origin goodness right in the heart of the East End in Bethnal Green.

Just a few years ago, Phil was an innocently sugar-addicted radio producer, munching through cheapo bars in BBC radio studios. Then he set out to travel in Central America, and in a cacao grove (or plantation, or field – the sources differ) he had what amounts to a chocolate-related epiphany and realised what his true course in life should be.

So he talked his way into some apprentice work with Paul A Young, gradually educating his palate and learning the ways of the professional chocolatier. He employed, we are told, an Indian spice grinder and a hairdryer to form his first bars by lamplight.

In 2015 the massively bearded and (in my opinion) tremendously self-important Mast Brothers rolled into London from New York, taking cavernous premises in the hipsterish zone of the East End and promising to take the capital's chocolate scene by storm. For various reasons they didn't do that, but while they were here Phil served as one of their makers and learned his skills well.

He took another trip – this time to Guatemala – to learn about harvesting and fermentation, and to discover new cacao varieties.

And then, in 2016, he looked around in East London to find a base of his own – and came across an old furniture-maker's workshop in Bethnal Green. Quite a lot of heavy lifting and painting later, he was ready to produce his own bars. And very, very good they are too.

I love the look of Land bars – immaculate, elegant, smooth and almost undecorated, they are substantial rectangles of honest, well-tempered chocolate that pay proper attention to bringing out the flavours of their single origins.

At present there is no dedicated Land retail outlet, but Phil's bars can be found in branches of Sourced Market and other enlightened chocolatiers, through Cocoa Runners and on his own website.

He has also recently been asked to produce custom bars for a Michelin-related venture in the capital – recognition at the highest level that is entirely justified.

A word also for Lucocoa, who have been making bean-to-bar chocolate in the capital since 2014, and going down their own route as far as sweeteners are concerned. Amarachi Uzowuru, a former Students Union official and Comic Relief worker, and Andy Clarke, a sports journalist, are the team, wielding their grinders in North London. Their bars, made in small batches, are sweetened only with unrefined coconut sugar and a 'superfruit' from Peru called lucuma (hence the company's name). Well worth a try.

One of the places where you can pick up Lucocoa's bars is a remarkable enterprise in one of London's most characterful areas, the Chocolate Museum in Brixton.

Don't think on the scale of the Natural History Museum, or the Science Museum, or the British Museum. Think smaller. Think a great deal smaller; in fact, rather more on the scale of two basement rooms, which is what you will find just off Brixton's main drag.

This fine little operation which, with total justification, bills itself as 'London's only chocolate museum', is an adjunct to a self-effacing little chocolate shop on a Brixton side street – which is itself an offshoot of a (slightly) more ambitious set-up in the more distant southern suburb of Peckham. The total absence of commercial puffery is charming, and a huge contrast to the bombast of Cadbury World (and indeed the massively bearded Mast Bros).

The little Brixton museum is only open to the public on Wednesday, Thursday and Friday afternoons and at weekends. On Mondays, Tuesdays and mornings it is used – hurrah! – as a resource by local schools. But the resources – wall panels and artefacts – don't talk down to their audience, whatever their age.

There is a clear and dispassionate account of the history of cacao, cocoa and chocolate, and a lovely little collection of vessels for the consumption and sale of chocolate, from ancient Central American artefacts, through Victorian tins, to the Black Magic box delivered, in the spoofy television ads of my youth, by a kind of sub-James-Bond figure.

I arrived soon after opening time on a Wednesday but already there was a little gaggle of Dutch visitors downstairs poring over the china pots and cups from Victorian chocolate houses, and a pair of Australians upstairs choosing from the hot chocolate menu.

An incredibly friendly lady at the counter told me about the displays and enthused about an upcoming app, and then sold me a couple of bars of Duffy's from the limited but top-quality range of bars that they stock.

Among these are loosely wrapped bars from Melange, the parent shop/cafe/ brand in Peckham, founded and run by Isabelle Alaya. Hot chocolate is her most celebrated product – the Australian visitors raved about theirs – but I thought her coffee and aniseed milk bar was delicious.

It might all be a little on the ramshackle side for some, and by the standards of shiny, busy, ultra-commercial London it seems almost innocent. But I love this little museum, and the enduring passion and concerns of those who run it, and the chocolate they make. It won't change your life, but it could enrich an afternoon – and it should make you smile.

☐ One of London's most distinctive chocolate sensations – copied all over the world – is the sea salt caramel truffle, almost a chocolate cliché, but invented originally by Artisan du Chocolat for Gordon Ramsay back when the confident Scot was running just the one restaurant, and actually cooking there. That original choc – sweet, salty caramel in a dark chocolate shell – remains a little globular masterpiece.

☐ As we have seen, actually making chocolates in London is rare and bean-to-bar makers are few indeed.

TASTING NOTES

☐ Rococo are best known for pretty and delicate filled chocolates which make a wonderful and distinctive gift (do lots of tasting while you choose). Their flavoured bars – hints of herb and tea, and flowers – have passionate devotees, but I must say I incline towards the single-origin bars that they import from the Grenada Chocolate Company, especially the dark/sea salt, which I find incredibly moreish.

☐ Dom Ramsey's Islington shop has closed, and Damson Chocolate is on hold for now. But Dom continues work as a consultant, and I'm sure that he will be making own-brand chocolate again soon. You can follow him on Twitter at @DomRamsey.

☐ Land Chocolate make a small range of very good-looking bars; I am particularly fond of their 75% dark from the Philippines, sultry and characterful. Others swear by their gentler malted 65%. You decide...

WHAT DO I NEED TO BE A BEAN-TO-BAR MAKER?

Determination, dedication, passion – and one or two pieces of essential kit. The finest bean-to-bar chocolate makers on the planet started out on a tabletop with little more than enthusiasm, and you can join their ranks.

Here, with acknowledgements to Dom Ramsey (whose book *Chocolate* is highly recommended reading), are all the elements you really need when starting out.

THE KIT

ROASTER

A domestic oven will do very nicely. Spread your beans out on a standard baking tray in one layer. Dom recommends that you start out by roasting your beans for 20 minutes at 140°C, then taste; adjust subsequent roasts up or down in a range of 120–160°C and 10–30 minutes until you arrive at a flavour that seems right to you.

GRINDER

Not to be confused with the gay dating app of a similar name. This is the heftiest item in the bean-to-bar maker's kitchen – and it grinds and conches cocoa beans into what is effectively liquid chocolate over a period of many hours or days.

If you are looking to make small quantities of chocolate in a domestic kitchen, Dom Ramsey recommends a tabletop wet grinder, of the sort which is commonly used in India to prepare dosa.

Suitable machines can be found online. As to which is best: go to a chocolate fair or farmers' market and talk to your local bean-to-bar maker!

HAIRDRYER

Not a vanity purchase, but one of the most important items in the chocolate maker's armoury. A hairdryer is useful in two stages of the process – winnowing, in which the maker separates out bean shells from cacao nibs (cold air from the hairdryer gently blows away the lighter shards of shell, leaving the nibs behind); and tempering (hot air from the hairdryer is used to melt – and re-melt – chocolate until the correct texture is achieved).

MARBLE SLAB

Optional, but one of the trademark items of the serious chocolate maker. A marble slab is the ideal surface for tempering — cool so that it instantly reduces the temperature of molten chocolate, and smooth so that the chocolate can be easily worked around the slab. If you want to see how it is done the professional way, there is an excellent 'Tempering Chocolate' video by Paul A Young on YouTube. Suffice to say that you don't HAVE to end up covered in the stuff, though that always seems to happen to me.

DIGITAL FOOD THERMOMETER

Very important for temperature control when tempering your chocolate. Dom recommends one with a prong, and no sniggering at the back please.

MOULDS

Flexible plastic moulds in basic shapes are available online and at all cookshops to form your chocolate, after tempering, into its final shape. If you step up your production you might like to invest in professional polycarbonate moulds from specialist websites and suppliers.

WRAPPING

Every small-scale chocolate maker's secret nightmare, if we are being honest. A real fiddle, but unavoidable. Some claim to get trance-like about it; others bribe their children to do it. Machines are expensive and complex, and you still have to watch them like a hawk. A cunning solution — pioneered by Pump Street in Suffolk and also adopted by Heist in Wales — is safe-seal envelopes.

THE RAW MATERIALS

COCOA BEANS

Of course, the most important ingredient of all. Buy the best that you can afford, even when you are starting out – it is hard to assess your progress if you are using second-rate ingredients. Bags of 1–2kg are available online from specialist wholesalers, and you can also find bags – and talk to importers – at chocolate fairs and food festivals.

York Cocoa Works (yorkcocoahouse. co.uk) is a great source of excellent beans in a variety of packs from 200g upwards – brilliant for experimentation, and not madly expensive.

COCOA BUTTER

This smooths chocolate and makes it easier to work with. Again, available from wholesalers online in pellets or slabs.

CANE SUGAR

You can use refined sugar, but unrefined is much more in keeping with bean-to-bar chocolate, and simply tastes better.

MILK POWDER

If you are making milk chocolate, obvs. Choose an additive-free product, and not the stuff intended for babies.

ADDITIONS

Sea salt, chilli powder, freeze-dried fruit powder, nuts… but best to work out what you are doing with basic bars first, as inclusions complicate the chemistry.

That's it. Good luck!

And don't forget to send me a sample…

MANCHESTER

A CITY UNITED IN GOOD TASTE

USEFUL INFO

Dormouse Chocolate
Unit 0, Deansgate Mews
Great Northern Warehouse
Manchester M3 4EN

dormousechocolates.co.uk

At the southern end of Deansgate,
opposite Hilton Manchester Deansgate.

By train: If arriving by mainline train at Manchester
Piccadilly, hop on the No.2 free bus and get off
at Deansgate Station; many trains are also direct
to Deansgate from other destinations

Open: Wed–Sat 12–5pm (allows Isobel and
Karen time to make and package chocolate)

Pollen Bakery
Cotton Field Wharf
8 New Union Street
Manchester M4 6FQ

Open: Wed–Fri 8am–4pm;
Sat–Sun 10am–4pm

Cocoa-Cabana
168 Burton Road
Manchester M20 1LH

Open: Mon–Sat 10.30am–6pm; Sun 11am–5pm

Has been known to stock bars from the exceptionally good Vietnamese tree-to-bar maker Marou –
highly recommended. Check with them before visiting: **info@cocoa-cabana.co.uk** or **0161 282 5700**

THE DORMOUSE AWAKES

When I think of artisanal food and where it is made I think first of all of a cottage, somewhere deep in the country. A place of timeless Olde English charm, part *Country Life* cover photograph, part Harry Potter Hogsmeade village. In the cottage kitchen, where smoke drifts under low beams, I envisage an apple-cheeked and perhaps rather stout lady labouring mightily at a solid wooden table with a range – an Aga or Rayburn – cluttered with pots and pans in the background, and a ginger cat contentedly asleep in a ray of sunlight on the window.

Outside that window, I'm sure I can make out some of the animals who provide the raw materials for the hefty cook to work with, leading a picturesque and placid existence: hens pecking at grain in the farmyard, perhaps, while a Jersey cow or two lows gently in the green field beyond.

The reality of chocolate manufacture, even on a small scale, is not like that: largely for health and safety reasons, which would rule out the cluttered Aga, the smoky ceiling – and the cat.

Even if the maker is blessed with a rural location, actual production is likely to take place in a stripped-down industrial unit of a kind that is yet to grace the pages of *Country Life* or a Harry Potter film set.

The reality chez Dormouse in Manchester could not be further from such bucolic fantasies. The shop is down the modern-day equivalent of a back alley – a first-floor-level 'mews' over the road from a brand-new Hilton hotel and bang opposite a smart cinema.

The window at the back of the chocolate kitchen looks out not over cattle-speckled meadows but across the roofs of buses on Deansgate in the direction of the distant and far from picturesque River Irwell. One floor down is a row of lively boutiques at the southern end of one of the city's most frenzied shopping streets.

One of Dormouse Chocolate's next-door neighbours is an axe-throwing centre – no, really – and on the other side is a virtual reality adventure playground.

In between the two is Manchester's only specialist high-end chocolate shop – which also happens to be Manchester's only bean-to-bar chocolate factory. Here, surrounded by whirring grinders and throbbing conchers, flanked by a vast illuminated portrait of Hilda Ogden and huge hessian sacks of cocoa beans, are Isobel Carse and Karen Hughes, sole proprietors – and indeed sole employees – of Dormouse Chocolate.

It's not anyone's idea of a rural idyll, but this Dormouse is a different beast from its country cousin – a thriving business that was born and has grown up in the heart of the Manchester metropolitan area. Perhaps the only romantic aspect of the Dormouse story is how these beautiful bars came to be made in Manchester in the first place.

"Well…" Isobel admits with a laugh, "I came here for a night out, met Karen, and I never left…"

How she came to be making chocolate is more prosaic, though with equally happy results. As a student, Isobel got a part-time job in a branch of Hotel Chocolat. To start with she was selling chocolate – and I'm sure that with her genuine enthusiasm for the product she was very good at that – but before long a job came up on the production side, and Isobel proved to be a natural. Soon she was an in-house chocolatier, demonstrating techniques in prestige branches in High Street Kensington, Covent Garden and Edinburgh, at a time when the company was keen to attract customers at high-profile locations with a talented young chocolatier mixing up marvels at the counter.

Dormouse Chocolates
Bean to Bar
72% Dark Chocolate

Head office took note, and soon Isobel was posted to the development kitchen at HC's HQ in Huntingdon (see entry).

But the urge to make chocolate in her own way and on her own terms proved too strong, and Isobel and Karen set up Dormouse in December 2014, initially working from home and making truffles and bars in the kitchen.

To begin with, she admits, they were 'just messing around', but as Isobel decided that her focus should be on bars rather than truffles, it also became clear that the kitchen manufacturing space, while economical, had its practical drawbacks. Not least, as Karen notes, "that we had to clear everything away and clean down every time we needed to use the table for something else. Such as supper…"

Luckily, while Isobel is the specialist chocolate maker, Karen's skill set includes an impressive radar for a promising space, and the negotiating skills to secure such a space for a competitive rent. So Dormouse moved to the former canteen space at Granada Studios, and were soon making waves far beyond.

Dormouse made a big impact at the Chocolate Show in London, and could shortly boast to their starry neighbours at Granada that they were Academy award winners, having scooped the prize for UK Rising Star at the British Academy of Chocolate celebrations in 2017.

They found that working at Granada Studios provided them not only with a constant supply of curious customers, but also plenty of entertainment on the side.

"I was putting the bins out one night, and there was all this terrible screaming," recalls Karen. "I looked around a bit and asked someone what was going on. 'Oh you don't want to worry, love,' they said. 'That's just the League of Gentlemen carrying on.'"

"It was a lovely place to work," says Isobel, Karen's partner in work and life and the chief chocolate maker at Dormouse. "Although the canteen space was no longer feeding the staff and was in use by little start-ups like us, they were still making programmes there and there were all sorts of random people popping in and out. Great fun."

But short-lived, alas. Redevelopment – rampant throughout Manchester – did not spare the studios and Dormouse and all their fellow start-ups had to move on. They had plenty of notice, though, and Karen, something of a property whiz, patrolled the area for a new spot, soon coming across a row of street-food premises in a new development just down the road at Deansgate.

"Perfect," she reported back to Isobel. "The landlords are looking for interesting tenants, it's a brilliant space and it's right opposite the Odeon, so we'll have lots of impulse buyers."

So the Dormice moved their nest, and brought with them the vast, mounted promotional portraits of Hilda Ogden, which at once remind them of where they have come from and broadcast to the casual visitor their cultural affiliations.

Hilda also accurately suggests a note of good humour. One of the many things that I love about Dormouse is their enthusiasm and willingness to explain what they do and why to would-be customers.

They are consistently keen to take their show on the road, and are a big hit at farmers' markets and food fairs in the Manchester area, as well as cherished stallholders at the regular Canopy Market takeovers organised by Cocoa Runners at King's Cross in London.

Isobel is a relentless innovator, and Dormouse often produce limited-edition bars to showcase a particular bean or production process: one such experiment, which had chocolate nerds chattering for weeks, was the Harvest bars.

For these, Isobel set out to prove a phenomenon that had been hotly debated by growers and aficionados for years: whether or not the skin colour of a cocoa pod (which can vary through a startling range) affects the taste of the beans therein.

Isobel went to huge trouble to obtain sufficient quantities of beans from pods with red and with yellow skin – all harvested from the same variety of cacao tree, in the same plantation, at the same time.

These she made up into Red Bars and Yellow Bars, each containing exactly the same proportions of cocoa and sugar, and each prepared in exactly the same way. The two bars were then distributed to keen connoisseurs (I was one – we couldn't wait) for back-to-back tasting.

The wrappers were identical, except in colour, and the bars when unwrapped were impossible for me to tell apart. And yet, when tasted – in the mindful, absorbed, competition-judge manner – I felt that the Yellow Bar was sharper, the Red a shade more mellow. Was this the psychology of the wrapper colours, or even the connotations of the names at work?

I couldn't say. But the difference in flavour between the two bars was absolutely unmistakable, a long-pondered theory was finally confirmed, and Dormouse's reputation as exciting chocolate makers was firmly established.

❝ One of the many things that I love about Dormouse is their enthusiasm and willingness to explain what they do and why to would-be customers

Their Toasted White, a mellow golden creation as far removed from the Milkybar as Manchester is from the moon, brings new subtlety and depth to a kind of chocolate that is often overlooked by 'serious' makers. It won huge admiration among fellow makers, a spot on the *Sunday Brunch* television show and a Gold at the Academy of Chocolate awards.

This and other fresh takes on chocolate traditions have won Dormouse an international reputation, rave reviews from *National Geographic* magazine and a rapturous reception from American food journalists when they flew over as honoured guests to a US chocolate festival.

All this attention might go the heads of those who are in it for the fame. But Isobel enjoys what she does and the two Dormice are in the chocolate business for fun. The evidence is not just the guaranteed smiley greeting I get whenever I march up to their stall at a fair or festival, but the humour they put into what they make.

Take Valentine's Day, for example, third on the list of marketing opportunities for any chocolate maker behind the jamborees of Easter and Christmas, and a date that most mass-market chocolatiers approach with a clichéd clutch of crimson or pink-dyed heart-shaped truffles.

Not Dormouse. Their justly celebrated Valentine's creation, an annual bestseller, is not pretty or cute: it is an anatomically correct human heart, asymmetrical, fed by arteries and flecked with veins, and executed in solid (and solidly delicious) single origin – last year it was Peruvian dark or milk, or Madagascan golden white.

A glorious, hilarious creation, and (if your intended is of a like mind to me) one guaranteed to win them over. Reactions I have observed include a scream, a close inspection and then a voracious bite that would have done justice to Christopher Lee in full Dracula mode.

There is wit in the flavourings of Dormouse bars as well – a festive take on the continental Christmas cake Stollen, for example, and an approving nod to the company's Manchester heritage with an upcoming 'cup of tea' bar – actually a milk chocolate infused with tea flavours, courtesy of the local (Chorlton) tea merchant Bohea.

Their latest, glorious creation is a bright pink bar of raspberry-tinted 'white' chocolate flavoured and 'crunchified' with maple almond biscuits. It's a hoot – and already much beloved by Japanese Instagram chocolate fans, of whom there are many.

Behind the fun, though, is a keen appreciation of technique and hours of close study of flavour and texture. Karen is coming along in this area – although she admits that when the company was getting started her appreciation was limited to the ability to tell dark from milk – but the dedicated student is Isobel.

On the day I visited the shop in Deansgate Mews she had been puzzling over a batch of beans recently delivered from Sierra Leone. "I've tried a few different ways with them," Isobel explained. "Different time conching, less sugar, more sugar, different kind of sugar. But it's not quite right yet. What do you think?" She handed me a chunk snapped off an experimental bar. Better than most of the chocolate I'd encounter in an average month, I thought. But I made a non-committal face.

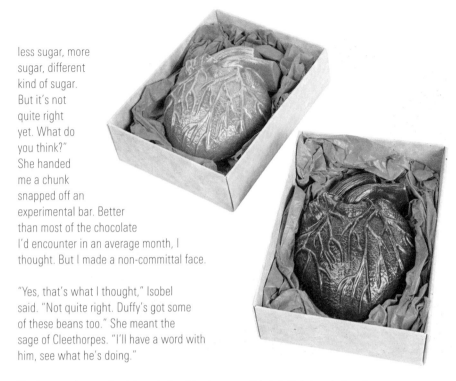

"Yes, that's what I thought," Isobel said. "Not quite right. Duffy's got some of these beans too." She meant the sage of Cleethorpes. "I'll have a word with him, see what he's doing."

That's a good example of the relationships between Britain's little band of craft chocolate makers. They are in constant competition for the best raw materials – and for the custom of a relatively small marketplace. But there's a federal sense of mutual support, an understanding that by pooling their knowledge in the pursuit of excellence they can all make progress together.

Besides, it can get a little lonely being a chocolate fan in Manchester. In many ways the city is ideal for a set-up such as Dormouse. There's a powerful and long-established food and drink culture (barm cakes, black pudding, beer and more) that has been turbocharged by the UK's artisanal food boom of the last few years.

The food scene is every bit as lively as the city's music, fashion and sporting environments. There are craft beer pubs, coffee roasteries and farmers' markets popping up all over the city and a vast audience of ethically aware consumers keen to try new taste sensations. It's just that chocolate doesn't feature very prominently, and never really has.

While Birmingham had its Cadburys, Bristol its Frys and York its Rowntrees, with offshoots of all three round about, in the early years of Britain's chocolate ascendancy, when our nation led the world in the industrial exploitation of the fruits of the cacao tree, Manchester had, in the local patter, bugger all.

So it remains. With the exception of Cocoa-Cabana, producing decent slabs and cakes up Didsbury way, and Cacoa Elora, making fine bars a fair way off, Dormouse is pretty much it for decent chocolate in the Manchester metropolitan area. And it's not all that easy to get hold of their bars.

Perhaps wary of cannibalising sales in their own shop, Dormouse do not flood the city's retail community with their products. In fact, at the time of my visit, the only place apart from their little shop where you could buy their bars over the counter was the lovely bakery called Pollen in Ancoats, over on the other side of the city.

This is a set-up not unlike Pump Street in Suffolk, demonstrating once again the affinity between good baking and serious chocolate making. As at Dormouse, the opening hours at Pollen are limited, to allow the baker/proprietors to spend an appropriate proportion of their time on making good things as well as selling them.

Given their dedication and imagination, it's not surprising that Dormouse are doing well – perhaps it's more remarkable that at present they have the field to themselves. They are certainly not complaining. And their fame is spreading far beyond Manchester and its suburbs. As far as the upper reaches of Switzerland, in fact.

" In the early years of Britain's chocolate ascendancy, when our nation led the world in the industrial exploitation of the fruits of the cacao tree, Manchester had, in the local patter, bugger all

A couple of years ago I got a text from a good friend of mine who works in the television industry. Gerhard (we'll call him, for reasons of commercial anonymity) is something of a mogul in the TV business, with fingers in many international televisual pies, a near-constant travel schedule, and a bolthole in a beautiful and remote village high in the Swiss alps.

He was passing through London and at a loose end. What was I up to? As chance would have it, I was off to the Chocolate Show at the Olympia exhibition halls in West London, a frantically busy gathering of chocolate makers and chocolate fans from all over the world.

I was judging a competition at the show, and Gerhard was happy to tag along. As we walked around the thronged hall, tasting and chatting, he was captivated by the friendliness and enthusiasm of the exhibitors, and tasted dozens of free samples. He was particularly taken by the Dormouse stand – Karen and Isobel were exhibiting at the show for the first time, and explained something of their adventures to date as Gerhard nibbled one of their earliest award winners and prodded in wonder at a moulded chocolate anatomical heart, which he seemed to find oddly captivating.

Something about the scene appealed to him, and as we shared a taxi away from the show, Gerhard was busily collating the contact details he had gathered on his iPhone and making ruminative noises about Swiss dairy policy and high-altitude cooking processes.

A few days later he was on the phone to me from Seattle, or Tel Aviv, or Minsk, or wherever he was buying or selling programmes or movies or studios that week.

"I'd like to make some chocolate in my village in Switzerland," he said. "It's just what the place needs. Do you think the good ladies of Dormouse would help me out?"

I felt sure that they would. But don't the Swiss already make chocolate of their own?

"Lindt?" said Gerhard. "Pah. It's rubbish compared to that stuff from Manchester."

So Gerhard visited Manchester (rumours that, while there, he put in a bid for *Coronation Street* have been denied) and was given a crash course in the art of making a chocolate bar. He told Dormouse what he had in mind, and they told him what he would need by way of raw materials.

A certain amount of to-ing and fro-ing ensued, I am told, and there was some difficulty in transporting the necessary equipment up an alp aboard a mountain railway train, but experiments conducted in Deansgate continue and I have tasted a splendid prototype bar. It may not be long before chocolate connoisseurs are able to buy a bar made in Switzerland but conceived in Manchester. Meanwhile, make tracks for Deansgate.

The much-celebrated Toasted White is a Dormouse classic – last time I visited this was being made with 38% Madagascan and it's a mellow treat. Add a 60% Peruvian dark milk (so fashionable at the moment, your dark milk), a 70% Peruvian praline and a Guatemalan 72% dark and you have four fine examples of the bean-to-bar maker's art for £20. It's a steal.

Like all good bean-to-bar makers, Dormouse's range changes from time to time according to which top-quality beans they have been able to source recently.

TASTING NOTES

The anatomical heart is one of the wittiest and tastiest chocolate shapes on sale in the UK, and the website blurb is fabulous: *As Dusty once sang: 'Take another little piece of my heart, now baby'… but who knew it would taste so good?* I've enjoyed this in various flavours in the past – milk with wafer; dark with hazelnut; almond milk vegan – follow your heart… £8 or thereabouts.

☐ Cacoa Elora (the peculiar spelling of cacao is their own) make bean-to-bar chocolate in a village just outside Matlock, Derbyshire, gateway to the Peak District. I've given them their own mini-chapter because there aren't any other bean-to-bar makers (as far as I know) in their area, and it didn't seem fair to lump them in with Manchester, which is a fair way away and (frankly) not as pretty.

☐ John Cowings is the man behind the brand. A local authority professional, John is also dedicated to making excellent small-batch bars of single-origin chocolate in his home kitchen in his spare time, which he sells at food fairs and farmers' markets around the area. I have tried a good few of them.

☐ Check out the website (cacoa-elora.co.uk) for up-to-date offerings. Among my favourites are their characterful and forthright Guatemalan 68% Lachua, a confident bar made with beans from Uncommon Cacao that certainly lets you know it has arrived...

☐ His Bolivian 70% Alto Beni is another confident bar which compares very well with a bar made from the same source (at the same percentage) by Bullion in Sheffield. Expect Cacao Elora to go from strength to strength.

HUNTINGDON
(AND ST LUCIA – AND JAPAN)

AND TOMORROW... THE WORLD

USEFUL INFO

Hotel Chocolat factory outlet:

**Hotel Chocolat Hadley Park Factory Shop,
3 Redwongs Way, Huntingdon PE29 7HF**

Open: Mon–Sat 10am–5:30pm; Sun 11am–1pm

**Hotel Chocolat Covent Garden,
4 Monmouth Street, London WC2H 9HB**

Open: Mon–Fri 8am–8pm, Sat 10am–8pm,
Sun 10am–7pm

**Hotel Chocolat Rabot 1745
Restaurant, Café and Shop,
2–4 Bedale Street, Borough Market,
London SE1 9AL**

020 7378 8226

borough@rabot1745.com

Open: Shop: Mon–Sun, 9am–6pm
Cafe: Mon 8am–6pm; Tue–Fri, 8am–5.30pm;
Sat 9am–5.30pm; Sun, 9am–6pm
Bar: Tue–Sat, 5.30pm–late
Restaurant: Tue–Fri noon–10pm
Sat 9am–10pm.

At the time of writing Hotel Chocolat
had approximately 170 outlets of various kinds in the UK, including about 30 cafes and more than a dozen Schools of Chocolate, where you can learn tasting and making skills from trained chocolatiers.

For a full and updated list of all stores and services, go to **hotelchocolat.com**

To find out more about the actual Hotel Chocolat in St Lucia, go to
hotelchocolat.com/uk/boucan/the-hotel.html

HOTEL CHOCOLAT

Every Wednesday morning at 10.30 in a large modern building on the outskirts of Huntingdon, a meeting takes place which has considerable significance for the chocolate lovers of Great Britain.

Half a dozen people sit around an immaculately clean table. In front of each of them is a napkin, an empty cardboard cup with a lid and a small number of shiny chocolates or squares of chocolate. At each place there is also a pair of laminated cards roughly the size of a paperback book cover. One of each pair is red, the other green.

A trim man of middle years with longish blond hair and a subtle suntan brings the meeting to order. "Right," he says, with a trace of a northern accent and a wide, white smile. "What do we have to look forward to this morning?"

The man is Angus Thirlwell, chief executive and co-founder of Hotel Chocolat, a company that has no close equivalent anywhere in the world and which is worth in the region of £100 million. The meeting is the weekly tasting and evaluation session for prospective new products, in the experimental kitchen at the company's factory.

It is a very select gathering and its deliberations are a closely guarded secret. I have been accorded the extraordinary privilege of attending, on condition that I do not reveal the precise nature of the products that are there to be assessed.

In front of us on the table sit the very latest creations of the dreamers, engineers, scientists and all-around chocolate fanatics on HC's staff. Some items that might appear on the table are the fruits of Thirlwell's chocolate-oriented imagination. Some are versions of existing favourites. Some have been suggested by shop-floor staff from the company's retail empire – and some have been suggested by customers, either in the shops or via the Tasting Club that HC has run for many years.

Around us as we taste, chefs and boffins work to refine yet further recipes in the test kitchen: treats for another day. The boss calls us to order. He is an affable figure, but he takes his job, and his chocolate, very seriously indeed: this is to be no chocolate gorger's jamboree.

Fashions in management practice come and go: you'll have heard of top-down firms, of trendy devolved organisations, of hands-on bosses and of management by walking around. But Angus Thirlwell has a technique all of his own. He runs a hugely successful international business by getting his hands on chocolates.

Not just his hands, of course. Thirlwell sniffs chocolate, snaps it, strokes it, stares at it, and then – only then – tastes it. And then he spits it out. Even if he likes it.

He has to. Hotel Chocolat is Thirlwell's company. With his business partner, Peter Harris, he founded the company more than 15 years ago, and the pair of them still run it. If Thirlwell had swallowed every chocolate he had tasted in that productive decade, it is unlikely that he – or the company – would still be in such great shape today.

Most of Thirlwell's chocolate tasting takes place on Wednesday mornings at Hotel Chocolat's factory on the outskirts of Huntingdon. There, he and the company's development team gather once a week to taste every single new item a number of times before it gets anywhere near a box or display case in one of Hotel Chocolat's shops.

It's a democratic process – the team vote with red or green cards, before any discussion – but Thirlwell's is the constant, guiding voice, the embodiment of the brand and guardian of its values as he has been ever since the first shop opened in Watford in September 2004.

Why Watford? "We didn't want to start out anywhere flash," he explains to me after the tasting session. "The whole point right from the start was to bring the best of the best to the widest possible audience. Starting out in Knightsbridge would not have been right."

Thirlwell recalls watching with his colleagues as the first customers arrived. "We weren't total novices," he says. "We already knew what people liked to buy online. But in a shop, we had to find the right line, to be exciting and escapist without being too rarefied. I remember standing in the shop with my wife the night before we opened, wondering if we had got it right. We were pretty anxious."

> 66 I was trying to come up with something that expressed the power that chocolate has to lift you out of your current mood and take you to a better place

The experience that the small team had built up with their mail-order chocolate business, Choc Express, proved invaluable in providing insights into the tastes of the British public and how best to package chocolates. Even so, they gave the shop a full year to prove itself through the peaks and troughs of the calendar.

"We wanted to be sure it was resonating," Thirlwell recalls. "To be sure that people were coming back, and not just on Valentine's Day, at Easter and at Christmas."

They were, and soon the unusual name was cropping up on more malls and high streets. Ah yes, the name: in the early days, there was no hotel as such… "It was aspirational," Thirlwell explains. "I was trying to come up with something that expressed the power that chocolate has to lift you out of your current mood and take you to a better place.

"And the French spelling came from that wonderful book by Joanne Harris, and of course the film version. Once you have seen and heard Juliette Binoche say 'chocolat' you never forget it…"

These days, as well as 100-plus shops in the UK (and more, as we shall see, elsewhere), there are smart restaurants and cafes, hands-on chocolate-making experiences, a cocoa-butter-based beauty range and the hotel itself, sited right on the cocoa plantation in St Lucia that has become the spiritual home and physical expression of the brand.

"That was something we always wanted to do, it just came about rather earlier in the lifespan of the business than we were expecting," Thirlwell confesses. "A member of our chocolate Tasting Club sent me a copy of an old book called *From Plantation to Chocolate*. I took it with me when I went to visit my father, who lives in the West Indies. Then, serendipity, this place in St Lucia came on the market and I thought: 'This is what we've got to do next.' "

The acquisition and restoration of the old Rabot plantation, and the evolution of the hotel, spa and restaurant in St Lucia, have been hugely significant. It allows Hotel Chocolat to call themselves 'cocoa grower' as well as 'chocolate maker', a key point of distinction, and it affords valuable insight into every stage of the production of their raw material, so that not only can they experiment with the effect of microclimates to produce site-specific bars, they can also see eye to eye with their suppliers and ensure the prices they pay and the support they offer are effective. All of which feeds back into the shops.

Rabot 1745 – the date refers to the establishment of the estate – has developed into a smarter sub-brand within Hotel Chocolat, adorning its most upmarket chocolates and meaning that customers initially lured by HC's reasonably priced bonbons can move up the scale to a box of 'single côte' Rabot 1745 truffles made from the fruit of trees in one particular area of the estate, and then on (pausing only to slather on cocoa-based beauty products) to a table at the restaurant and – for the privileged few – a visit to the real Hotel Chocolat.

If you are at present unable to contemplate a stay in one of the hotel's 14 luxurious suites, you can get a literal taste of what it is like at Hotel Chocolat's Boucan restaurant overlooking Borough Market in London, where the kitchen replicates recipes from the hotel's head chef. The restaurant's decor also features elements taken from the hotel – and lumps of the island's flora.

Tabletops in the upstairs dining room and the ground-floor cocktail bar are made from highly polished ironwood, felled by hurricanes rather than profit-hungry humans. Concrete and corrugated iron also feature, helping to give the visitor something of the plantation vibe and bring them closer to the spiritual home of the company and Caribbean cuisine.

Thirlwell visits St Lucia as often as he can, and not just to kick back in the bar or chill out in the spa. He will be found all over the estate, talking with the people who work there about growing conditions among the trees, or fermentation processes for the beans – and sharing with them some of the latest experimental products from Huntingdon, looking for feedback on the chocolate from the people who grew the beans.

He also travels outside the estate – Hotel Chocolat has gone beyond the revival of cacao growing on its own property to encouraging farmers elsewhere on the island, and the label 'St Lucia Island Growers' on its bars is one that the entire community is glad to see.

Integrity is a word that is much bandied around in foodie circles, but in the competitive world of high-class chocolate, it is generally reckoned Hotel Chocolat has it. The company listed on the stock exchange a couple of years ago, but Thirlwell and Harris remain very much in charge, and looking to invest in growing their business rather than diversifying away from it.

The potential for smugness and indulgence is obvious, yet Thirlwell is manifestly grounded. In his early 50s, he lives with his wife, Libby, and their grown-up children near Cambridge. He enjoys sailing and driving his old Porsche.

More often than not, though, he's thinking about chocolate, and in the assessment session that I joined in the development kitchen, he led all the discussions about flavour, texture and appearance. When we came to raise our laminated cards to signal approval or disapproval of each item that was up for tasting, all eyes were on Thirlwell's card.

My access to the tasting session was a great privilege, but fans of the company's products can get involved in such decisions more easily than they might know. The company runs a Tasting Club that anyone can join. For a fee you get early examples

of chocolates that Hotel Chocolat is thinking of bringing to market, and you can express your views online.

You are also guaranteed at least a modest free taste at any of the company's branches when you pop in. And there are plenty to choose from.

I wondered which of their branches I should feature in this book: a large and shiny pavilion of deliciousness? An airport or mainline station booth? A full-range chocolaterie with an upscale restaurant attached? In the end I decided to visit one of the smallest branches, but perhaps one of the most significant, just inside the factory gates on an industrial estate on the outskirts of Huntingdon in Cambridgeshire.

It is miniature – no larger than the tiny branch of HC at Victoria Station – but it is served by an enormous car park (which doubles as the car park for the factory's staff) and it is very popular with the more clued-up of the company's customers, who realise that very good chocolate can be picked up here at the very keenest of prices.

I visited on a blisteringly cold day in early February, and a steady stream of fans arrived and made a beeline for the Christmas range, glorious goodies with a month to go on their 'consume by' dates now discounted by 50% or even 70% simply because they were shaped like snowflakes, Santas or festive conifers.

On the other side of the store, not discounted but as fresh as can be, sat the very latest fruits of the production line, the earliest of the Easter eggs.

So an unusual store, but also an important and informative one. It is located here because the factory is here. But why is the factory here? For the same reason why so many of Huntingdon's buildings are.

There is nothing romantic about the chocolate factory's position. It is fairly close to Angus Thirlwell's home, but that was not the deciding factor. The deciding factor was its prime position for distribution purposes – adjacent to the A1, close to where that becomes the A1(M), and therefore close to the nation's motorway network and all of HC's UK shops.

The 20-minute walk from the train station reinforces the point about connectivity. At the station, mainline trains linking London with Leeds and points further north thunder through on the central tracks as my commuter train pulls in. The A14 trunk road crosses the track almost above the platforms, and the multi-carriageway A1 flies simultaneously over both.

Between the station and the old town there is a strip of development typical of a southeastern community: traffic lights and a short strip of road adjoin a wasteland that signs announce as the forthcoming 'Falcon Quarter' – you won't see many major developments in England these days that aren't some kind of quarter.

Buildings next door to the 'Quarter' will become another block of retirement flats to accompany those that already nestle next to the Aldi supermarket. So far, so bland: this might be Baldock, Bletchley or Brackley. My instructions say to turn left at the green Chinese, and almost immediately right. This is where the town becomes more interesting, and not only for the revolting paint job on the Cantonese cafe.

The multiple layers of burnt avocado emulsion on the side wall of the restaurant can't conceal the ghostly attachments of a long-demolished outhouse or – it occurs to me – stable… because surely this was once an inn.

And so, now that I come to look at it, was the building on the other side of the road, which boasts a remarkably ornate pillared porch. On the far side of the Chinese, as

I walk along the pavement, I come to an arched passageway leading behind the buildings, which may have led once to yards where coaches could be fettled and horses changed.

And attached to the wall of a smart row of well-kept (surely Georgian) houses opposite is the final clue.

The street sign identifies the thoroughfare as Ermine Street, a stretch of one of England's most important Roman roads, leading from Bishopsgate, one of the entrances to Londinium, north to the cities of York and Lincoln. The road was named, not for the slinky animal that provided fur for ancient gowns, but in a corruption of the name of the ancient English tribe who lived hereabouts before the Romans arrived, the Earningas.

So the road and the buildings around it have been staging posts and supply points for more than two thousand years, and what drew Hotel Chocolat here is what drew the innkeepers, ostlers and market traders in the ancient past: proximity to England's arteries.

There are traders here still, and not just in the factory outlet – in the marketplace on Saturday a butcher's lorry has drawn up, next to the pop-up bouncy castle, and one side of the vehicle has dropped down to reveal slabs of steak and stacks of burgers.

Across the way an enterprising food stall offers a range of dishes that would have fed the most demanding and cosmopolitan of legionaries: 'Mediterranean Style Chinese Food', the blackboard read, elaborating: 'Chilli, Tava, Sweet & Sour, Sweet Soy, Katsu Flavored Chicken Meals! Gluten Free! Vegan! No MSG! Halal!' No box unticked.

I resisted, and wandered on. Huntingdon is a combination of the picturesque and the bland: an exquisite, empty church facing the closing-down sale of a discount shoe shop; Molby's hairdresser neighbouring the Norman façade of a tiny museum. It feels, like so many towns surrounded by arterial roads, as if it has been thoroughly bypassed.

All the excitement, for the chocolate hunter, is on the fringe, where a band of neat estates (pampas grass shivering on California Road; breeze-block extensions with mock-Tudor paint jobs) gives way to well-tended allotments and an electricity substation and there – suddenly filling the view in low-rise monochrome splendour – is Hotel Chocolat's smart and very substantial factory.

At this point I had better try to explain how it is that Hotel Chocolat fits into this book. It is clear that the company is not an artisan chocolate maker. The factory makes a million chocolates a day, and that cannot be achieved entirely by hand. Humans are involved, especially in quality control, but the immaculate Huntingdon production lines consist mostly of shiny machines engaged in a relentless chocolatey ballet.

It remains, though, a human company on a human scale. I have spent many hours with staff at every level of the organisation in a wide variety of locations (and I am a regular paying customer at a wide variety of branches) and I have never met anyone involved at any level who does not believe in what they are doing.

Hotel Chocolat is a company of chocolate lovers. It may have developed in a thoroughly modern manner – they were doing online sales before Amazon – but at heart the operation is based on growing chocolate, buying beans that are ethically sourced, making good things with those raw materials, and selling them at accessible prices.

The company may now be listed on the stock market with a valuation in the region of £100 million, but the major shareholders are still the people who founded it, not a vast, faceless multinational. It is an independent British chocolate company that goes about its business in a decent way with good intentions, that helps cocoa growers abroad in practical ways, and that is by far the most powerful ambassador for good chocolate that this country possesses. That's why they are in the book.

One more thing that HC has in common with other, smaller-scale makers is that everyone seems to enjoy what they are doing. Go into any branch – whether a 100sq ft pop-in at a train station or a lavish

5,000sq ft barn, and you will be swooped upon by a smiley staffer bearing a tray of free samples.

This is good. But what is better is that the staffer will know what they are offering. They will know how it is made, they will know where the ingredients have come from, and they will have tasted it themselves.

This level of knowledge and engagement is intensified further up the organisation, so that when I have visited the factory, and especially the development kitchen, I have been consistently astonished at the depth, breadth and sophistication of knowledge that I find.

Angus the CEO clearly exemplifies this (and his founding partner, Peter Harris, knows as much about effective retail siting and strategising as Angus does about chocolate) but the team who invent and perfect the chocolates and bars that the company sells are as amiable a bunch of chocolate nerds as you will ever come across.

When our tasting session was over, the room reverted to its usual role as an imaginarium and proving ground for the creative notions of the company's chocolatiers. When Angus bounces back in from the Caribbean with a hint of a tan, a glint in his eye and some beans in his pocket, it is the team in the development kitchen (also known as The Invention Room) who will be the first to hear what he has on his mind. For all the joys of communing with the growers on the ground, it is what happens in here that will convert the beans into joy – and cash.

> For all the joys of communing with the growers on the ground; it is what happens in here that will convert the beans into joy – and cash

Adam Geileskey is the company's Head of Development, and one of the most entertaining and knowledgeable people on the UK chocolate scene. He has rescued me many times when I have needed a technical explanation for why a particular kind of chocolate tastes the way it does, or why some ingredients react better with chocolate than others.

He is very much at home debating chemical, culinary and ethical issues at an academic conference, but equally comfortable suggesting refinements to the giant – and staggeringly effective – chocolate sculptures produced by one of his most gifted and versatile colleagues, Rhona Macfadyen.

One of Rhona's recent triumphs was a life-sized likeness of an English bulldog, named Mr Nibs and shipped, with great care, to the site of Hotel Chocolat's latest high-profile store opening – in the Aeon Lake Town shopping centre on the outskirts of Tokyo.

Mr Nibs provided a clearly irresistible opportunity for Japanese fans to take selfies with an unusual English icon – but opening a store so far from home also provided a chance for Angus Thirlwell and his team to learn something from the Japanese attitude to chocolate.

"The Japanese have a much less complicated relationship with chocolate than perhaps we do," Angus tells me soon after the store opened. There's no guilt there,

it seems. And in any case that is an emotion that Thirlwell believes is unwarranted in regard to good, high-cocoa, low-sugar chocolate. Instead, Hotel Chocolat's Japanese customers "know they deserve it, they want it – and they are getting it".

In return, Angus and the dozen HC staff who travelled to Japan to set up the shop received a range of insights into the Japanese work ethic, retail style and food culture. He took 'hundreds' of photographs and a pile of notes that he has been working through back in Huntingdon.

I'm likely to first encounter the fruits of this research at one of Hotel Chocolat's seasonal launches, which often take place at their shop in Covent Garden in central London. The premises are well suited to these jamborees, with extensive space upstairs for displaying new products, and a cellar downstairs with a bar fully stocked with chocolate-related liqueurs.

All of this – along with a fully functioning conch machine and extensive space for demonstrations and education – is open to the shopping public every day, and only sequestered for the media's benefit at launch times.

Just as the fashion world is fixated on key seasonal dates for the launch of individual collections, so major food retailers aim to have their new products ready for the market well ahead of the most important sales dates on the calendar.

Hotel Chocolat's most important sales periods are, in ascending order of importance, Valentine's Day, Easter and Christmas. The romantic festival does not get a launch of its own, but journalists with notably soppy audiences may be sent a sneak preview of heart-shaped scarlet treats ahead of time.

Easter justifies an egg-themed takeover of the Covent Garden store and much discussion among the assembled media of the intricacies of ovoid mouldings and the niceties of shell thickness. Beau Bunny, the company's slightly disturbing tuxedo-clad, rabbit-headed promotional character, is sure to make an appearance.

But Christmas is The Big One, and in order to fit in with the long lead-times of glossy magazines, Hotel Chocolat holds a Christmas in July when distinctly unseasonal 'snow' will drift over the shelves, and guests will hurry home with Santa figurines in danger of melting; then it all happens again in October for broadcast, online and newspaper journalists.

Certain media figures (ahem) may insist that they should attend both: any excuse to talk Caribbean plantation innovations with Angus, shop locations with Peter Harris, and the latest flavour combinations with Adam Geileskey. Rhona Macfadyen is always on hand, casting anxious glances as people queue up to be photographed with her latest giant sculptural creation.

Other independent UK chocolate makers are not so wedded to the calendar, but the Hotel Chocolat team always rise to the occasion, even if they are not always entirely sure what the occasion is. At Christmas – even Christmas in July – they are often thinking about the next Easter, and at Easter they will be well advanced with preparations for the following Christmas, or the Easter after that.

Now, with a store in Japan and more planned there and in the United States, fresh celebratory opportunities open up. We may not see cherry-blossom-themed truffles or Thanksgiving chocolates on British high streets, but we can share a sense of national pride that an independent British chocolate maker is spreading the love of cocoa – and a proper respect for the people that grow it – around the world.

☐ I'm not going to recommend individual filled chocolates because the range changes fairly frequently and everyone has their own favourites. I am happy to admit without shame that I am partial to an Eton Mess on a festive occasion, which is nothing at all to do with my taste in friends and quite a lot to do with my fondness for a sticky, sweet and only vaguely chocolatey confection from time to time. I am human, after all.

☐ The title of this book is *From Bean to Bar* and it's important to point out that Hotel Chocolat are, alongside everything else that they do, bean-to-bar chocolate makers (with ambitions to become tree-to-bar makers when their St Lucia factory is up and running).

TASTING
NOTES

☐ HC's single-origin bars are extremely good value compared with mass-produced junk, and you can taste your way around the chocolate world for a modest outlay.

☐ Their bean-to-bar, single-origin range is most often to be found in the display area of their shops designated 'The Selector', where customers can mix and match small packets (often of six filled chocolates or two decent-sized bars) and buy them for £3.95, or three for £10.

☐ In the Selector range but perhaps of less interest to chocolate purists are the nutty, fruity bars that are an immense source of pleasure to my colleagues — and a very useful tool for weaning yourself, or any misguided friends, away from ghastly mass-produced gunk.

☐ Look out for the bars that come from the Rabot Estate in St Lucia — these are Angus Thirlwell's pride and joy. They are beautifully made and quite distinctive. Those from a certain area or *côte* on the estate are even more exclusive.

☐ Of the other single-origin bars, I'm personally a big fan of the Cienaga bars from Colombia, and a dark milk from that range (say 65% cocoa) is one of my regular choices for gentle, delicious, undemanding 'comfort' chocolate.

I have found Hotel Chocolat's peanut butter bar highly efficacious in turning those hopelessly addicted to the sugary abominations known as Reese's Pieces on to more virtuous paths. The same is also true of the variety of fruit and nut bars in the Selector range, all of which are better made, with infinitely better chocolate, than the high street bars of the same name made by You Know Who.

My most ardent Hotel Chocolat recommendation is to have a look at joining their Tasting Club. For a subscription (currently £22.95 a month), you receive a box through the post every month of bars and/or filled chocolates tailored to your tastes. At present you can choose from Mellow, High Cocoa, Fortified (ie boozy), Classic and Rare & Vintage.

I have long been signed up for the Rare & Vintage box, and it brings me regular treats from the wilder fringes of the Hotel Chocolat experience – single-estate bars, bars with experimental inclusions, a packet of dried fruits enrobed in a rich bean-to-bar coating, a clutch of roasted but unshelled cacao beans, and so on. All kinds of weird and wonderful things, and I happen to know from talking to Angus and Adam that such items are often 'auditioning' for inclusion in the general range.

Tasting Club members – there are more than 50,000 – are always asked for their opinion on what they have been sent, and their feedback is tremendously important in deciding the line-ups that will be found in future Hotel Chocolat collections. Get involved! hotelchocolat.com/uk/shop/tasting-club/join

DORSET
FAMILY VALUES

USEFUL INFO

Chococo Swanage
21C Commercial Road
Swanage
BH19 1DF

By car: Much your best bet, really. There is a car park in Mermond Place, off Station Road, a 3-minute walk away from Chococo.

By train/bus: Or you can travel by train to Wareham (on the mainline from Southampton and London Waterloo); the No. 40 bus goes hourly to Swanage from outside Wareham Post Office; the journey takes about 30 minutes and costs from £3; a taxi for the same journey will cost £35–£40.

Chococo Winchester
152 High Street, Winchester SO23 9AY

Chococo Exeter
22 Gandy Street, Exeter EX4 3LS

Chococo Horsham
42a Carfax, Horsham RH12 1EQ

Chococo mail order and online: **chococo.co.uk**

Solkiki do not have an actual shop or cafe and put all their energy into chocolate making.

But their website is excellent and highly informative about their methods and beliefs.

If you are vegan and a chocolate lover, I highly recommend visiting **solkiki.co.uk**

LIVING THE
BEAUTIFUL DREAM

As with houses, the retail guru's mantra for shop, restaurant or cafe positioning is 'Location, Location, Location'. This suggests that premises too far off the beaten track or too distant from other similar businesses will have little chance of success. So a retail guru would surely be baffled by the location of the beating heart of the Chococo empire – if, that is, the guru could find it.

First of all, the guru would have to get to Swanage, which is in itself no mean feat of navigation. It is not so hard to get to its near-neighbour, Poole, which is bursting with metropolitan confidence and contains, on its smartest fringes, some of the most expensive residential properties in the UK, or the bustling near-city of Bournemouth, even closer to Swanage and boasting a university and an airport. But the shortest link between these places and Swanage is the chain ferry, which seems to spend most of its time under repair.

Without it, the traveller must trundle along the marvellously scenic but extraordinarily twisty A351, a road that is mysteriously popular with the owners of delightful but arthritic vintage cars which find the frequent ascents challenging in the extreme.

The A351 leads onto the Isle of Purbeck, not an island as such but with all the attitude of one, including a feisty sign at the border with the real world. Guarding the route to Swanage is Corfe Castle, an astonishing stump of medieval military might that was comprehensively blown up by Cromwell's troops during the English Civil War, a slight which still disgruntles the locals.

Assuming the retail guru can tear themselves away from the limitless selfie opportunities of Corfe, they will soon be in Swanage and the hunt for Chococo will begin in earnest. They will look in vain on the seafront, though they will no doubt enjoy the fabulous views of Studland Bay and Old Harry Rocks, with the Isle of Wight looming on the horizon. Nor will they find a wonderful chocolate shop and cafe on the main drag, though they would be forgiven for popping into any number of intriguing little independent emporia.

Instead they should press on through the town to Station Road, which leads to the wonderful retro train terminus, whose wonderful retro trains are not (of course) connected to the national network. If the guru can bear to pass by the wool shop, Pet Luv and Burt's Bits, they might make a left turn onto a narrow street called Commercial Road.

Nearly there! Left again at the old Quaker meeting house, then right up a cobbled alleyway, bollarded against traffic – and there the guru would at last find Chococo's chocolate house and cafe, in a location that even Chococo's co-founder, Claire Burnet, admits is 'ridiculous'.

Yet this hard-to-find gem is one of Swanage's proudest boasts, with star billing on the tourist leaflets and a reputation that brings visitors not only from all over the town but all over Dorset and from much, much further afield.

Upstairs in the cafe, beside the children's play area, is a wall map of the planet and plonked upon it are stickers denoting all the places from which travellers have

visited. The confetti sprawl of international blobs declares that for all the obscurity of its location, Chococo has turned out to have truly global appeal.

The cafe, now lovingly described by staff and customers alike as the 'mothership' of the burgeoning little Chococo empire, was established in this initially unpromising spot by Claire and her husband Andy in December 2002. "Just before Christmas," Claire notes, "which tells you how much we knew at the time."

Claire set about making chocolates on the ground floor, while the cafe set-up upstairs was "another daft idea", which meant that whenever a customer came in she had to leave off truffle-dipping and gallop upstairs to serve.

They sent out an exploratory mailshot, offering handmade chocolates filled with locally sourced ingredients, and received 175 orders, from friends and relatives, and friends and relatives of friends and relatives, which Claire thought was great – until she realised that she had no idea how, or in what, she was to pack the chocolates for delivery.

> ❝ The cafe, now lovingly described by staff and customers alike as the 'mothership' of the burgeoning little Chococo empire, was established in this initially unpromising spot by Claire and her husband Andy in December 2002

With the last Christmas post looming, Claire appealed for help to her sister, who drove down from London for an all-night epic of folding and sticking and labelling.

All was well. The chocolates were delivered, the customers loved them, and repeat orders flooded in.

The same formula, with a vastly expanded range and environmentally friendly improvements to the packaging, still holds good today, though Chococo's original premises have quadrupled in size, spread over the road and been joined by three more shops/cafes in much more sensible locations across the south of England.

Production has moved on somewhat as well, from Claire and Andy rolling and enrobing and blobbing on the ground floor to an expansive factory in nearby Wareham, home to 20 or so of the company's 70-odd staff.

The essential philosophy, and the essential appeal of the chocolates, remains exactly the same: treats that are made with care by people who enjoy what they are doing and take pride in it – treats that involve as many local ingredients as possible, and that ensure that all raw materials are sourced with the wellbeing of the communities that produce them in mind.

Let's look at a box of Chococo's finest. The chocolate comes from people who know their growers well, and pay them properly: people who Claire and Andy have visited and worked with for years. The fillings include honey and honeycomb from hives in the garden of the cottage next door to the Burnets' home, where they have lived all the while that Chococo has been thriving.

The cream in the ganaches comes from Trevor Craig, "the last dairy farmer in South Dorset who delivers" and the booze in the chocolates is local too – Twisted Nose gin, Black Cow vodka. The chocolates look wonderful – smooth and shiny and colourful – but there is no messing around with the ingredients, no weird chemicals for colour, sheen or preservation – and that last point is important.

Chococo makes fresh chocolates. Not the kind that can be left around to gather dust and then raided in desperation a couple of months later. The kind that must be eaten soon after they are purchased or received, which is not something that customers find difficult to achieve.

Up at the factory in Wareham, properly bedecked in white coat and hat for sanitary purposes, Claire leads me into the production area to show me how these little wonders are made. Emma, the first staff member we meet, is experimenting with a new peach ganache, trying to find the right level of that fruit's elusive flavour in bowls of melted chocolate from a variety of origins. It is a pleasure to dip a clean spoon into each just-set mixture and consider her efforts. Claire decides that Emma is not quite there yet: I beg to be left alone a little longer with the bowls to consider that matter further, but Claire moves me on.

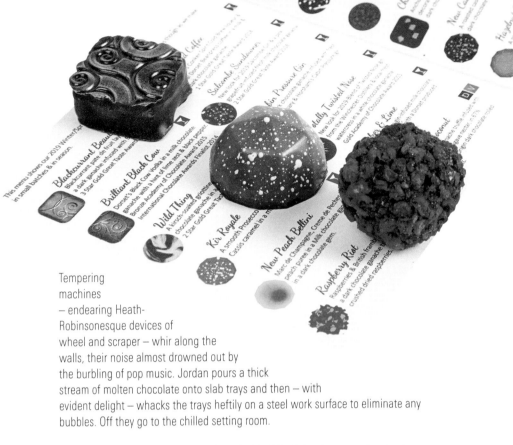

The menu shows our 2019 WinterSpring in small batches & in season.

Blackcurrant Beauty
Blackcurrant pate de fruit layered with a dark ganache infused with black pepper
3 Star Gold Great Taste Award

Brilliant Black Cow
Dorset's Black Cow Vodka in a milk chocolate ganache with a hint of lime zest & black pepper
Bronze Academy of Chocolate Award 2015
International Chocolate Awards Finalist 2014

Wild Thing
A kirsch-soaked griottine chocolate ganache in...
2 Star Gold Great Tast...

Kir Royale
A smooth Prosecco...
Cassis caramel in a m...

New Peach Bellini
Marc de Champagne, crème de Pêche...
peach purée in a Milk chocolate g...
in a dark chocolate gem.

Raspberry Riot
Raspberries & British framb...
a dark chocolate ganache t...
crushed dried raspberries...

Tempering
machines
– endearing Heath-
Robinsonesque devices of
wheel and scraper – whir along the
walls, their noise almost drowned out by
the burbling of pop music. Jordan pours a thick
stream of molten chocolate onto slab trays and then – with
evident delight – whacks the trays heftily on a steel work surface to eliminate any
bubbles. Off they go to the chilled setting room.

Nearby, Jackie is – now what exactly is Jackie doing? On closer examination, it
is clear that Jackie is flicking a paint-laden toothbrush at a table populated with
chocolate orangutans. Of course she is.

Jackie is Chococo's decoration whiz, and the orangutans, who are all called either
Tuan or Tuantoo, are to be sold in support of the Sumatran Orangutan Society to
help rebuild the rainforest in which the endangered creatures live. "They're selling
really well," Claire reports. "SOS have planted 140 cacao trees with our help
already." Orangutans, apparently, love cacao trees. And Jackie is having a great
time speckling chocolate orangutans with her toothbrush. It's a virtuous circle, of
a slightly peculiar kind.

Next door to Jackie, Dan is sticking fish together. He is a dapper figure with a
neat beard and an engaging smile, and he is an absolute genius at uniting the
two halves of a chocolate fish – or ammonite, or dinosaur or, for traditionalists,
Easter egg. This is a skill that is little recognised among the chocolate cognoscenti

> **All that I need to do, Emma explains, handing me a bag like an udder filled with ganache, is squeeze and lift… squeeze and lift… squeeze and… "Oh dear."**

but, when you come to think about it, one that is central to the enjoyment of many of our favourite chocolate treats. Easter eggs do not spring into life fully formed: they are not, no matter how delightful it may be to imagine, laid by chocolate birds.

An egg, or any substantial hollow chocolate shape, is made by moulding it in two halves (or, for really complex shapes, more elements) and then sticking them together. And the only way to do the sticking – at least in an artisanal set-up – is by hand.

So Dan gently releases two halves of the six-inch fish – an elegant tribute to Chococo's seaside base – from the their moulds and then places them, edge down, on what appears to be a Hostess plate warmer. "That's because it is a Hostess plate warmer," he explains, before plucking them up after no more than a second or two, placing their slightly molten edges precisely together and, with one smooth movement, swiping any excess from the seam before laying them reverentially nearby to firm up.

"Do you want to have a go?" he asks. "It's not difficult…" I can tell that it is, though, and I can't bear the thought of messing up those lovely fish, or blowing up the plate warmer, or melting myself…

Claire has a better idea. "Come back to Emma again," she suggests. "You can do some piping."

This sounds safer. Emma is a nice lady and piping is something that I have seen many times on *The Great British Bake Off*. What could possibly go wrong?

Emma is piping ganache – the delicious yet basic mixture of cream and chocolate that is at the heart of many soft centres – into almost spherical blobs an inch or so in diameter and half an inch apart. The blobs are created in long ranks on trays which will soon go into the cooling room before employment in lovely filled chocolates.

All that I need to do, Emma explains, handing me a bag like an udder filled with ganache, is squeeze and lift… squeeze and lift… squeeze and… "Oh dear."

Into Emma's immaculate line of near-identical spheres I have interspersed three floppy elongated cones which teeter for a moment and then collapse onto the tray like a trio of – I'm sorry about this but the resemblance is irresistible – dog's willies.

"No, really, they're very good," Emma insists, taking back the bag and demonstrating once again. "Perhaps you should think about giving the bag a little twist as you finish off and then they won't be so… limp."

Gamely, I have another go, but we both know that the attempt is doomed. I get the feeling – not uncommon when I am let loose in a chocolate factory – that I am an awful lot better at consuming chocolates than I am at making them.

So I am much more at ease a short while later, back at the mothership in Swanage, sipping a mug of frothy hot chocolate made with 75% Tanzanian flakes and nibbling at a nutmeg praline while Claire explains what brought her and Andy into chocolate – and into Swanage – in the first place.

Claire and Andy were both working in established industries (she in consumer marketing, he in tech) when the urge to do something on a more human scale began to creep up on them.

Claire had also taken a year out to sail around the world with the BT Global Challenge, which equipped her with invaluable knowledge about team building and crew morale, a healthy sense of self-belief – and an element of fearlessness.

"We were living in West London and we noticed a little chocolate shop there," Claire recalls. "Then we'd come down here at the weekends and talk and think about ways that we could move down here full-time and find something more rewarding to do with our lives."

Andy had inherited a little cottage in Swanage from an elderly relative, next to the lifeboat station and with a glorious view over Studland Bay. The couple's first child was starting to toddle and Dorset seemed to be a healthier place to raise a family than the noisy, busy, polluted capital.

"We were talking this kind of thing over one weekend and nibbling on some chocolates and we said, 'Mmmm. These taste all right, but we could maybe do better...'"

When she was growing up, Claire and her family had lived for a time in Belgium, and that country's food culture, particularly in relation to chocolate, made a profound impression.

"I remember that in our local supermarket, there was a wall of chocolate bars, and in each case there was a label saying where the cocoa had come from. Now, when I think about it, I'm sure that some of that was down to Belgium's former involvement with colonies in Africa, but I thought at the time that it was fascinating that chocolate could come from all these different places."

The hot chocolate was made from real chocolate, young Claire noticed, and was served with cream from local farms... and dinner often came in the form of dishes ready-prepared by the local traiteur, again making use of ingredients from suppliers in the area.

"My mother was what would now be called a foodie, but back then it just meant that she cooked proper meals from scratch, and sent us to school with lovely things like chicken liver risotto in a Thermos flask, rather than sandwiches."

> " We were talking this kind of thing over one weekend and nibbling on some chocolates and we said, "Mmmm. These taste all right, but we could maybe do better..."

The legacy of this upbringing is a deep respect for the importance of fresh food made with the best possible local ingredients... and a recipe for chocolate biscuit cake which has been on the menu at Chococo cafes since the earliest days, and remains there now.

"Yes, that's my mother's recipe," Claire acknowledges. "I pimped it a little bit, but essentially that is still hers..."

Clearly this was a family of chocolate lovers, and between them they could not help but notice how sugar-laden the hot chocolate was when they moved back to the UK, and how rubbish the chocolate was compared to what they had been eating in Belgium.

Brief digression: I have done a great deal of dedicated and delicious research on this topic, and it is my firm conviction that there are now more makers of good chocolate in this country than there are in Belgium, and that the term 'Belgian chocolate' has become marketing shorthand for 'slightly posher than ordinary'. The Belgians' most celebrated brand, Godiva, is now owned by a Turkish company and produces shiny chocolates that seem most at home in the duty-free zone of an international airport. This is not to say that there are no interesting or worthy Belgian chocolatiers – Pierre Marcolini is a decent chap and makes some of the best hot chocolate that you can find in London – but I would contend that there is no justification for the shimmer of glamour that attaches to the phrase 'Belgian chocolate', and I don't see why we shouldn't be a lot louder in our celebration of the qualities of Proper British Chocolate. Rant over.

Where was I? Oh yes, in the Chococo cafe in Swanage with founder Claire. The amazing thing is that, after realising that they could do better than a lot of the chocolate they had come across, Claire and husband Andy actually set about proving it.

"I was feeding my baby daughter Lily at that time," Claire recalls, "and like any new mother I was concerned about what she was eating. So when we started to look at making chocolates, we were concerned straight away with traceability."

Their concern to use as many local ingredients as possible for fillings meant that they could keep a close eye on quality, but applying the same standards to chocolate was not such a straightforward process. Claire had to insist with suppliers that they give her as much information as they possibly could about the origin of the beans she was buying, and the conditions under which they had been grown.

They started out with El Rey in Venezuela, and as the business has grown, so has their web of trusted suppliers, both around the mothership and at the cacao end of things.

Growth has been slow, though: this is not the kind of set-up that proceeds through dramatic takeovers or swashbuckling profiteering.

"By the end of the first year, we had a website," Claire smiles, as if that recollection suggests the pace of business in a distant, primitive past. "The thing is, in order to grow, you need good people, and it can take time to find the right ones. This is a labour of love."

As has already been suggested, not many people would choose to set up a retail business in a back alley, off a side street, in a seaside town distant from major transport links, with absolutely no passing trade whatsoever. In winter.

"Ah yes," Claire acknowledges. "Some of that doesn't sound too clever. But some of it was actually an advantage. You see, we're countercyclical."

Swanage, as an English seaside resort, is a summer town. Of course the vast majority of the population live there all the year round, and most of the businesses tick over quite well through the winter, but the economic boom times are related to warmer weather and visiting families. On the day that I visited, in early January, all the shops were open and people cheerily greeted Claire as we swalked through the town, but the crazy little Jurassic Golf Course on the seafront was firmly shut.

But a cold day in England is a good day to be selling hot chocolate, and buying chocolates that won't melt on the way home. When the rest of Swanage is heaving with people, Chococo does just fine: the alleyway fills up with bodyboards, and bodyboarders fill up with chocolate ice cream. But in winter it does even better, because people love to buy chocolates for Christmas, and for Valentine's Day, and for Easter. That means that they thrive just when the local economy is under pressure: they are countercyclical.

That in turn means that when Chococo needs some extra help — part-timers to wrap chocolates, or make deliveries, or serve in the shops — there are plenty of people looking for the work.

All of this also underlines one of the reasons why England, and other seemingly unlikely countries such as Iceland and Denmark, are so well suited to the manufacture of chocolate.

This is a substance that, in its final form, melts at the temperature of the human body – or the temperature of a typical afternoon in West Africa, or Central America, or Southeast Asia, or anywhere else along the band of three degrees either side of the Equator which covers the only areas on the planet where cacao trees can grow wild or be successfully cultivated.

So in the earliest days of the manufacture of chocolate bars, the best places to make and sell them were countries with a naturally chilly climate, and that remains the case to this day.

There are companies that manufacture chocolate that is justifiably called 'tree to bar': that is, chocolate that is made close to where the beans that go into it are grown. Chocolat Madagascar – an important supplier for Chococo – is one, so is Menakao, also from that remarkable island, and Marou in Vietnam.

But on the whole it is easier to make chocolate in a country where your factory – and, perhaps more significantly, your warehouse – does not require significant air conditioning. And it is certainly easier to sell it in such a country.

It is challenging enough for a small-scale manufacturer to invest in equipment that will keep their finished chocolate bars in good condition while they are on their own premises. But it is difficult, if not impossible, for them to mandate all of the circumstances under which their goods can be sold: a warm shop is the enemy of good chocolate.

All of these circumstances made England an ideal location for the earliest exponents of mass chocolate-bar manufacture and retail. Add to the convenient climate the right kind of retail space at the right price, a market of customers well disposed towards local producers, a network of keen suppliers of delicious ingredients, and a pool of job-hungry workers, and it is clear why Swanage is not such a loopy place to set up after all.

Over the last 17 years, Claire and Andy have managed to find plenty of the right kind of people to help them make Chococo work. The company now employs 75 or

so staff, and there are three shops as well as the mothership, not to mention the thriving online orders despatched from the factory in Wareham.

The other shops are in Exeter to the west, in the remarkably chocolatey city of Winchester (see 'The South'), and in Horsham in Surrey to the east.

Growth has been careful and gentle, undertaken at a pace that all concerned feel is comfortable, and not driven by pushy shareholders or demanding banks, but by a sense that a new space in a new place just feels absolutely right.

Chococo have stayed close to their original suppliers, too. Among the soft centres on display in any branch of Chococo you will always find at least one or two that feature honey or honeycomb from Bob's bees — known to an appreciative public as Robert Fielding Honey, but to Claire and Andy as their next-door neighbour in the cottages overlooking Studland Bay.

"We've brought people along with us," Claire said. "A lot of the people who supply us have done so for years, like Bob." It has been the same when they have opened a new retail space, exploring the area around the new shop for new people to work with, people whose values and products fit into their ethos and meet their standards. "In every shop, for example, we work with a different coffee supplier local to that space." It's a kind of benevolent networking that builds businesses – and makes friends.

Another benevolent process is the gentle art of chocolate education, undertaken by all the staff at Chococo and spread among customers by a kind of good-spirited osmosis.

Courtney was behind the counter in the Swanage shop the day that I called in, and helped me select my edible souvenirs. "You must have some of the MegaMilk," she insisted, picking up a bar of Madagascan dark milk with a beautiful rich brown shade. "It's awesome. I love it so much."

Claire beamed to hear this. "When Courtney joined us," she pointed out, "she thought that chocolate meant Cadbury's."

This kind of gentle conversion has also worked farther afield. Like many chocolate makers, Claire runs tasting courses with a multiple purpose: to spread the word about the chocolate she makes, to entertain potential customers, and to educate them.

"I remember I once did a tasting for a group of people from a bank. They were on a corporate awayday and I was the sort of cabaret at the end." Claire got all of her wares set up, and then asked her audience if any of them liked chocolate.

"This lady jumped up and yelled 'Me! Yes, me! I'm the chocolate champion! My personal best is 24 Cadbury Creme Eggs at one sitting!'"

A lesser chocolatier might have been cowed by the challenge, but Claire has faith in what she makes, and by the end of the tasting the magic had worked. "That same lady came up to me and said, in a much quieter voice: 'Oh Claire, you've changed my life. I'm never eating another Creme Egg again.'" Heartwarming.

Chococo were one of the companies that helped fuel a great surge in Dorset pride – not only in the county's food, but also in its local identity, landscape and culture. Think of Dorset Blue Vinney cheese, Dorset knob biscuits, Dorset apple cake, the Duchy of Cornwall's old-style new town at Poundbury and the new-found worldwide fame of the Jurassic Coast and its fossils.

The good vibes are still spreading, and new ventures popping up where they are felt. At Thornford, near Sherborne, Bob Spink and Iris Stork are making chocolate in a way that reflects the spirit of Chococo but has a passion and commitment that is all their own.

I first came across Solkiki Chocolate at the Chocolate Show in London, a festival that is currently dormant but which for a few years was a wonderful melting bowl of talented chocolate makers and chocolate fans. Word got around that there were new makers on the scene with a distinctive take on ethics and processes, and the cognoscenti were soon besieging their stand.

> " I love what they do and what they make, and the way that they go about it: full of enthusiasm, friendly, approachable and keen to share what they make and what they know

Iris is a trained clinical psychologist and Bob was a creative director in the games industry. They met in Iris's native Netherlands and discovered fine-flavour ethical bean-to-bar chocolate together in San Francisco in 2008. They continued to experiment with beans, flavours and moulds, and when eventually they decided to move, with their two children, back to Bob's native Dorset in 2014, they resolved to build their future around their own kind of chocolate-making business.

They found a characterful cottage/workshop amid beautiful scenery to make their home and base and set to work.

Since their debut Bob and Iris have quickly built an international reputation, winning more than 60 awards for beautiful bars made with a passionate commitment to ethical excellence, with a respect for a vegan lifestyle, but also with masses of fun and imagination and a vast range of flavours and cocoa origins.

I love what they do and what they make, and the way that they go about it: full of enthusiasm, friendly, approachable and keen to share what they make and what they know.

Iris has been vegan for more than two decades, Bob for more than 10 years, so it made perfect sense for them to make chocolate without any animal ingredients.

"Making chocolate without dairy brings its own challenges in the recipes and in the flavours," Iris admits. "But finding alternatives for making milk and white chocolate is a fun challenge on its own. We always strive to make the best-tasting chocolate we can possibly make. If it's not the best we've ever tasted in our lives then we don't see the point – we set the bar (no pun intended) really high."

Their aim is to make exceptional chocolate for everyone – specifically including those who prefer to embrace a vegan lifestyle and who have profound concerns about the way in which the food they eat is produced.

"We want to improve the lives of those around us, and leave the world a better place," Iris says. When it comes to the beans they use, the search for high quality dovetails with their ethical approach. "The only way you can consistently find high-quality cacao is when the cacao is consistently well farmed, fermented and looked after during the entire process," Bob explains. "This can happen when the farmers are motivated by being rewarded well financially for their efforts."

They trade directly, which means they know where the beans have come from, and where their money is going. And they try, gently and with humour, to explain how and why they do what they do to their customers – both on (and inside) the recyclable packaging of their bars and at the fairs and chocolate festivals where they do a lot of their selling.

Their attitude – and their story – has a lot of parallels with the early days of Chococo. And it is still early days for Solkiki. "We are still a micro-business, since it's just Iris and Bob," Iris admits. "We started with a very basic shoestring budget and we're always playing around with food for fun. We go from strength to strength. It's been hard work, but very rewarding and great fun!"

Their cottage premises is powered exclusively by renewable energy, and Iris and Bob insist that "no planets, people or animals are harmed" when they make chocolate. These are worthy aspirations, but no joy is lost as a side effect, either in production or product. The main thing, after all, according to Iris, is to "leave behind only a trail of positivity and generate as many smiles around us as we can".

It is encouraging for the two of them that they can feel their philosophy taking effect, not just in the wonderfully chocolate-aware county they live in but further afield as well.

"The 'chocolate bug' is spreading," Bob declares. "People have been turned on to craft chocolate, we see them organising tasting evenings amongst themselves and with friends and there's a real response to our chocolate and a palpable excitement for it."

This kind of 'conversion' is a huge motivation for people like Bob and Iris who make chocolate in the right way for the right reasons. It is a motivation for me in writing this book, to reach out to people who have only ever consumed industrial chocolate. As Iris says, "It is a real privilege to explain and see people's eyes open and their taste buds as well."

That's pure Dorset pioneering spirit. So my advice boils down to this: if you haven't been to Dorset, go. If you go to Dorset, go to Swanage (and pause en route as you travel through Corfe, as you inevitably will, because it is insanely picturesque). Go to Chococo in Swanage (ask if you don't know the way – it won't take you long to find someone who does), order a hot chocolate and take your time building yourself a selection box of soft centres. Do talk to the staff about what you like – and what they like: they love to share what they know and what they love.

Remember what this customer emailed to Claire not so long ago, because while it is twee it is also not far wrong: "Chococo encompasses everything that is good in this world, wraps it in happiness, and delivers it with joy."

Can't get to Dorset? Go to Horsham, Winchester or Exeter, and proceed in the Chococo shops there as suggested above. Still stuck? Get online...

Don't like filled chocolates? Good grief. Why not? Sorry, I mean, try Chococo's MegaMilk bar, which is awesome, but also get online and check out Solkiki's amazing and imaginative range. This advice also applies if you love chocolate but are vegan, because Solkiki will sort you out with love and deliciousness.

Dorset? You can't beat it.

□ Chococo specialise in filled chocolates, so what you choose from their range will be a matter of taste as to what you like in the way of fillings.

□ If at all possible I highly recommend visiting one of Chococo's shops/cafes and tasting and talking. But if that is not an option and you'd like to explore their range at your leisure then a large tasting box is £22, from the website.

TASTING NOTES

□ In the face of all this soft-centred loveliness I can almost lose my focus on single-origin chocolate-bar excellence – but no one who is remotely interested in good bars should miss out on Chococo's MegaMilk, a warm-toned bar of 65% Madagascan cocoa that is one of the finest dark milk chocolates you will ever come across, and a huge favourite among my chocolate-loving friends.

□ Among Chococo's current range, my favourites include their classic dark sea salt caramels, made with smoked local sea salt, £11 for nine, and their truffles made with fresh Dorset cream – these have a shelf life of only two weeks, apparently. In my house they have never lasted more than a day.

☐ Solkiki make a wide range of vegan chocolate bars. They source beans carefully from suppliers they trust, and in many cases they enjoy long-term trading relationships. Availability of specific bars varies from time to time for the best of reasons, but among their bars that I have very much enjoyed are the following three...

☐ Marañón 60% salted caramel dark mylk, a sultry number made with Peruvian beans and coconut that is beautifully rounded and sweet without being remotely cloying – an absolute treat.

☐ Gran Chililique 70%, which has notes of fruit and flowers in a lovely gentle dark bar made with cacao from the Chililique hills in northern Peru.

☐ Kaithapara Vanam 71%, a lovely dark bar from India, is characterful and a good representative of this hugely promising new source of beans.

HOW TO TASTE CHOCOLATE

I know. Put it in your mouth and go nom nom nom.

That method works perfectly well with bog-standard chocolate, which delivers a big hit of sugary flavour and fatty texture and very little else. There is not a great deal to linger over, and it is not a substance that rewards careful consumption. Dwell on a Dairy Milk or a Galaxy or similar, and all you are likely to experience is a sugar headache, a claggy mouth and a lingering sense of shame.

But proper chocolate, made with fine ingredients by an expert and diligent craftsperson, demands much greater care and attention.

Of course you are welcome to enjoy your chocolate in any way that you choose, but I have found that I get more out of a bar when I consume it with my senses properly engaged. I am trying desperately to avoid the word 'mindful' here, but for once it may be justified.

If you have got hold of a bar of good bean-to-bar chocolate, it is worth taking your time to savour every mouthful. Here, compiled with the aid of the team at Cocoa Runners (cocoarunners.com), and with input from international chocolate judges, taste experts and all-around cocoa gurus Jennifer Earle (jenniferearle.com) and Hazel Lee (hazeljlee.com), is a guide to tasting chocolate properly.

Look at your bar

Is it smooth? Is it shiny? These would be good things. Warning signs to look out for include bubbles, swirls of a slightly different colour, and dusty or chalky deposits – the first two indicate poor tempering, the second two poor storage. Those deposits are likely to indicate fat that has risen to the surface when the bar has partially melted and then solidified again. Don't keep good chocolate in a warm place!

Break off a piece

Obviously, because you're not going to stuff the entire bar in your gob at once. But the way it breaks can give you a clue about quality: good chocolate breaks with a strong, even audible snap. You'll often see a chocolate judge break a bar next to their ear and murmur: "Mmm. Good snap." They may be a little self-conscious at such a moment (I know I am) but they are looking for a clean break rather than a limp or soft one, which would indicate poor texture or (once again) inadequate storage.

Sniff it

Good chocolate should smell of chocolate (bad chocolate smells of nothing at all, if you're lucky, and industrial fat if you're not). Really good chocolate might give you an aroma that suggests the origin of the beans – a hint of red or citrus fruit, perhaps

(Madagascar and Vietnam respectively) or a tang of tobacco (Indonesia). You are giving your senses a hint of what is to come: a lot of what you 'taste' is actually aroma released in your mouth.

Don't put it in your mouth...

... hold on a moment longer. Is the chunk melting smoothly on your fingers? Good chocolate contains cocoa butter, which melts at the temperature of the human body. Mass-market bars crumble into a sticky mess – because the manufacturers sell off cocoa butter to the cosmetics industry and replace it with cheap fat. Ew.

NOW put it in your mouth

But don't chew. Put the chunk on your tongue and let it melt. As the cocoa butter and the chocolate dissolve, different levels of flavour will be released. An initial hit of fresh banana may develop into a mellower note, or sharpen into citrus. Try to associate the flavours you are getting with other foods or aromas that they call to mind, no matter how weird they may seem. As your chunk melts, move it around your mouth; breathe in through your nose, and bear in mind that your sense of smell as well as your sense of taste delivers flavour, and that different areas of your tongue may pick up distinct flavour elements.

Take notes...

... if you are feeling nerdy. Hazel Lee (right) has developed a Tasting With Colour chart (see her website for details) that many aficionados find really useful for clarifying their tasting sensations. I have a chocolate-tasting journal (from Moleskine, the posh diary people, ultra-nerdy) with specialised charts and flavour wheels that I have found invaluable and which has turned into an extensive record of hundreds of bars that I have tasted down the years. I often photograph bars that I am tasting, next to their wrappers, and post them on Twitter. They may inspire other people to give them a go, and they provide a visual journal (with dates) of what I have enjoyed. You can have a look on Twitter at @ccAndrewBaker – ignore the posts about my daughters and my dog.

You might like to try tasting bars of the same cocoa percentage from different single origins – you will soon pick up the distinctive flavour characteristics of the many different places in which cacao is grown. I have found that round about 70% is a good benchmark, and also one that many makers employ.

... and... spit

Only kidding. Unlike wine tasting, it is considered perfectly acceptable to swallow chocolate that you have been tasting. It is true that Angus Thirlwell carries a paper cup when he is doing the rounds at Hotel Chocolat HQ into which he discreetly spits, but he is tasting multiple chocolates with multiple fillings and needs to keep his palate clear. You knock it back.

All of the above advice is optional

If you have gone to the trouble to find and purchase good chocolate made by good people in the right way, then I salute you, and freely concede that you can do with it as you wish. Stick it up your nose or smear it on the soles of your feet if it makes you feel good. But if you do choose to eat it with care, at least you now know how.

THE SOUTH

IT'S BEAUTIFUL

USEFUL INFO

Winchester is 68 miles southwest of London, just off the M3.

Drivers might also like to note the colourful bollards in the centre of town, painted in the styles of celebrated artists. They are, however, made of solid iron, so while they should not be missed, they should also be avoided.

Winchester is on the main train line out of London Waterloo and there are 132 trains a day between the two cities, with prices from £14 and journey times upwards from 1hr 58 min – so not exactly a high-speed line, but all the more time to savour your chocolate.

Brighton is at the southern end of the A23 and pretty much due south of Gatwick airport; frequent trains for Brighton leave from London's Victoria and Blackfriars stations.

Montezuma's Winchester

41 High Street, Winchester SO23 9BL

Open: Mon–Fri 9am–5.30pm;
Sat 9.30am–6pm;
Sun 10.30am–4.30pm

Montezuma's Brighton

30 Duke Street, Brighton BN1 1AG

Open: Mon–Sat 9.30am–6pm;
Sun 11am–5pm

Other branches in Kingston, Chichester and London (Spitalfields).

Chococo Winchester

152 High Street, Winchester SO23 9AY

01929 421777

Open: Mon–Fri 9.30am–5.30pm; Sat 9am–5.30pm; Sun 10.30am–5pm

Winchester locals prize the shop for its coffee and cakes as well as chocolates, and this emporium was voted both the city's Favourite Food & Drink Business and its Favourite Independent Business in 2017.

Winchester Cocoa Company

winchestercocoa.co.uk

Pop-up shop: Winchester Christmas Market, Cathedral Square

Winchester Fine Chocolates

winchesterfinechocolates.co.uk

You can order Zara Snell's delicious and beautiful chocolates (and check out her latest chocolate-based artistic creations) online at:

Twitter: twitter.com/zarasnellxx

Instagram: instagram.com/zarasnell

Better still, you can enjoy her chocolates as an amuse-bouche or end-of-meal embellishment to your dessert at Winchester's Michelin-starred restaurant, **The Black Rat: theblackrat.co.uk**.

J Cocoa

James Hull does not yet have his own physical retail outlet, though I first discovered his bars on the counter at Dormouse in Manchester. You can get them there, subject to availability, but the best bet is to go to James's website, **jcocoa.co.uk**

BURNT CAKES
AND FINE CHOCOLATE

Winchester, the ancient capital of England, should be on the must-visit list of any traveller in Britain for a host of reasons.

History lovers will want to pay homage to the historic seat of government and the old kings, where one of the country's most celebrated monarchs (and least talented cooks) reigned.

Students of architecture will marvel at the glories of the cathedral, one of the finest ecclesiastical masterpieces not only in England but in all of Europe, and fans of great literature and of a gentler age will want to pay their respects at the grave of Jane Austen, perhaps England's greatest novelist.

But chocolate devotees can send their companions off in search of these delights while they explore what has become a centre of innovation and dedication among makers of chocolate, a place boasting not only some of the nation's finest and most amply stocked shops, but some of its most innovative and imaginative makers.

Any dissent from the historically minded can be headed off by the confident assertion that the cakes that King Alfred burned have recently been subjected to carbon isotope analysis and were proved beyond a shadow of doubt to have been chocolate brownies. If challenged, say that it must be true because you read it in a book. Just don't say that it was this book.

I find it easy to get carried away with the superlatives when I'm talking about Winchester, one of my favourite little cities in the world. It is a wonderful place for the chocophile to visit with family and friends, because you can put together a deliciously rewarding itinerary that combines places of great general interest with pit stops for indulgent experiments in cocoa-based delight.

However you approach Winchester, the cathedral will be the first thing that you see. It is vast and ancient – the longest Gothic cathedral in Europe. Construction started on the building you see now in 1079, barely more than a decade after William the Conqueror first set foot in England.

But kings more ancient than William I ruled in Winchester – and have been commemorated in both stone and chocolate.

This was the seat of Alfred the Great, the first king of what we think of as England, a man infamous for burning the brownies that he had promised to watch for one of his subjects, but who was also a wise and courageous ruler who greatly advanced the culture and learning of his kingdom.

Alfred was memorialised in chocolate form by the West Country chocolatiers Chococo, who, when they opened only their second shop here, produced beautiful and vast 'gold' chocolate coins with Alfred's ancient image upon them – a wonderful treasure indeed for local children to find hidden under the Christmas tree.

Alfred really existed, but traces – somewhat doubtful – of a more shadowy historical figure can be found at Winchester Castle, where the Round Table of King Arthur, a convincingly vast circle of timber emblazoned with knights' names and medieval symbols, hangs on the wall of the Great Hall.

The symbols are the clue that it is a medieval fake – Arthur, if he is existed at all, was active in the Dark Ages of the 5th and 6th century, and the Round Table itself was a fabrication of much later storytellers. But it is a splendid object, and a good spot to savour a chunk of quality single-origin dark milk.

British rulers of less fame but perhaps greater power have issued forth from Winchester School, one of Britain's most exclusive, and most academically accomplished, private schools. Old boys are known as Wykehamists, and are famed equally for their acute intelligence and their lack of social aplomb. A reputation justified in both regards, based on those whom I have met.

Countless other fascinating footnotes to English history can be found when wandering the city's medieval streets, and you will not go short of quality sustenance while you do so. But enough! We are here for the chocolate.

> " I find it easy to get carried away with the superlatives when I'm talking about Winchester, one of my favourite little cities in the world

You really are spoilt for choice in Winchester, with rare outposts of two of the country's dedicated and ethically engaged chocolate retailers, a recent recruit to the ranks of innovative bean-to-bar makers, and a remarkably talented young chocolatier whose work is offered by Winchester's celebrated (and Michelin-starred) restaurant, the Black Rat.

We will come on to the chocolate makers in due course; first of all, Winchester has plenty to offer to the chocolate purchaser.

Concentrate your efforts on the High Street, which slopes gently downhill towards the river, with the wonderful bulk of the cathedral to one side.

Towards the bottom of the High Street, Chococo (eulogised in our chapter about Dorset) have one of their four branches, a cafe/shop of great contentment and an ideal pit stop after giving a polite bow – nothing too demonstrative – to the grave of Jane Austen in the cathedral.

Miss Austen did not mention chocolate in any of her works, which has not stopped an enterprising chocolate company producing a range of pretty products 'inspired by the world' depicted in her novels. These chocolates (of no great distinction, as

Lady Catherine de Bourgh might have put it) are made and sold in Edinburgh…
a city which is also absent from Jane's work.

I digress. Have a cup of single-origin hot chocolate at Chococo and then make your
way up the (largely pedestrianised) High Street. About half way up you will come
to the Butter Cross (or High Cross or City Cross), a striking medieval monument that
owes its dairy-related name to the practice of tradesmen selling butter there in
ancient times.

In slightly less ancient times (1770, in fact) the Butter Cross was sold by the
Winchester Paving Commissioners to a Mr Dummer, who was unpleasantly
surprised when the locals staged a small riot to prevent him from carrying it
off home.

It was cherished in typical can't-leave-anything-alone fashion by the Victorian
city fathers. They allowed George Gilbert Scott to 'restore' the cross, which is why
it looks as if the Albert Memorial has passed this way and inadvertently left its
toddler behind.

Anyhow, the Butter Cross is a handy landmark for chocolate fans, as it stands
beside a large store belonging to Montezuma's Chocolate, a worthy British
enterprise that has things in common with Chococo and Hotel Chocolat, and
to which we will return in more detail later in this chapter.

Buy a bar of two of Montezuma's (I am very taken with their dark chocolate and
chilli bar, especially in winter) and proceed up the High Street.

Around the point where traffic rejoins you will see the Old Fashioned Sweetie Shop.
Under normal circumstances I give this sort of place a wide berth as they tend to
be not nearly as old-fashioned as they claim, piling mass-produced sugary lumps in
retro-style jars and selling them at premium prices.

But I popped my head around the door this time and was drawn further in to an
interior that was narrow and deep and randomly recessed, the way that properly
old-fashioned shops often are. The shelves were crammed with weird delights from
all over the world that demanded further inspection.

It's true that this strangely compelling enterprise was no champion of local produce, and that quality and ethical considerations seemed low on its list of priorities. Bean-to-bar items, whether made in Britain or elsewhere, were nowhere to be seen.

But what a treasure house of sweet tat this was! No doubt the range of enticing junk could be sourced online with exhaustive effort, but there is something compelling about seeing an array of international goodies lined up within reach, tempting and touchable...

The majority of it was – to my fussy, elitist eye – sniggeringly awful: shiny rows of sugar-free chocolate bars from Spain and Belgium rammed with E numbers and heaven knows what else; vast slabs of peanut brittle; 'authentic' Turkish delight; Mike and Ike sour gums and American Milky Ways...

I made my excuses, battled past a throng of children besieging an unfortunate mother, and left. You might – if the virtues of properly made chocolate ever pall – find this place a useful antidote. I found it a valuable reminder of everything that I do well to avoid.

On a more virtuous note, two of the leading lights of Winchester's chocolate scene work out of the public eye, but they benefit from the synergies of a chocolate-loving city.

Chris Attewell founded the Winchester Cocoa Company just three years ago, and the business has zoomed to national fame and awards in double-quick time.

Chocolate judges and bloggers have been singing the praises of Chris's products right from the start and he is now expanding his original range to take in new flavours and carefully sourced new ingredients.

Chris has a plain but effective mantra for his enterprise: "The philosophy for our business is straightforward – keep things imaginative, authentic and simple," he said. "We create chocolates using natural ingredients and no artificial flavours or preservatives, giving them a less sweet and more natural flavour. Our chocolates are handmade in small batches and we source chocolate *couverture* that has been traded fairly (or, ideally, directly) and sustainably."

Couverture (from the French for 'covering') is the technical term for the chocolate that enrobes a truffle or other filled chocolate. Almost all makers of fine filled chocolates buy in their *couverture* from chocolate manufacturers, and the clued-up chocolate hunter will always ask a chocolatier where they source that most vital of ingredients.

Some makers of bean-to-bar chocolate (in particular Duffy Sheardown and Willie Harcourt-Cooze) work on a sufficient scale to supply chocolatiers with large(ish) quantities of chocolate for *couverture* work, at trade prices because of the scale of the orders, but with no compromise on quality.

Paul A Young, for example, the celebrated London chocolatier and television star, uses a lot of Duffy's single-origin bean-to-bar chocolate in his sumptuous truffles and other delights, and both of Winchester's excellent filled chocolate makers rely on top-quality suppliers.

> " Zara is one of the greatest young talents in British chocolate-making today

Both? Yes, because although the Winchester Cocoa Company make fine chocolates, they should not be confused with Winchester Fine Chocolates, which is the company founded by the hugely talented – and still remarkably youthful – Zara Snell.

Zara is one of the greatest young talents in British chocolate making today, having made an impact at the national and international level at an incredibly young age. Born and raised locally and still living in rural Hampshire, Zara is barely into her 20s yet has already won prestigious awards and worked with some of the most famous names in the chocolate business.

She first came to prominence when, while still a schoolgirl, she won the Great British Spiced Chocolate Challenge, a national competition, and, as one element of the prize, travelled to Grenada to visit growers and makers in the Caribbean.

One of the judges at the GBSCC was myself – but more significantly, another was Paul A Young, the ginger-haired genius of chocolate mentioned above, who invited Zara to work with him for a while in Soho to further her skills.

Zara is now back in Hampshire and making chocolates full-time. "I am in the process of designing a brand-new chocolate studio that will be built in my garden as I've outgrown my little cafe," she told me. "I'm hoping it will be complete before the summer, assuming that my boyfriend gets a wiggle on."

After her precocious early success as a teenager, Zara started to make filled chocolates for sale, initially working part-time while she completed her studies. She had the option to join any one of a number of established chocolatiers as an assistant, but instead chose to follow her own path, conceiving and executing filled chocs of great imagination and increasing technical difficulty with aplomb, all the while learning the boring but essential tradecraft of the small business owner.

At any chocolate fair where Zara was exhibiting you would find seasoned chocolate fanciers crowded around her stall, keen to try her latest inventions. I was invariably among them, and it has been a huge pleasure to see a rather shy schoolgirl developing into an accomplished and confident professional, even if the lady herself claims that it has all been a bit of a blur.

"I took the business full-time in July 2018, and it has been crazy from the off," Zara said. "We've been all over, exhibiting at chocolate fairs, music festivals, dog shows — you name it!"

The knack is to find the time to develop her craft while simultaneously selling her creations. "I'm always trying to develop new products and flavours — last year, for instance, I did a chocolate Advent calendar for the first time. So far this year I have developed a raspberry and gin truffle, a crunchy hazelnut praline and a locally sourced honey truffle, alongside some new bar flavours developed from some of the favourite Advent chocolates."

She is still supplying her local Michelin-starred restaurant, the kind of outlet that expert chocolatiers find hugely useful as a regular source of reliable income — and a shop window for their talents.

Zara is diversifying, too, improvising as climatic conditions demand: "Last summer I branched out with a range of high-quality brownies to get through the heat — I've had enough puddles of chocolate! These have proved really popular at music festivals and fairs, and they're going to take a front seat again this summer." The main thing, though, is that "I am still really enjoying myself".

Further east, on the fringes of lively Brighton, is the making base of another pioneering spirit, this time working on classical bean-to-bar production.

On the face of it, Brighton is the sort of location that you might expect to boast a horde of artisan chocolatiers. It is a fun, artistic, youthful and prosperous place — but there isn't a bean-to-bar cafe in sight.

In the centre of town is Koh-Koh, who proudly announce that all their chocolates are imported from Belgium. Why? When a few miles away the Winchester crews are turning out chocs for which any sane Belgian would top his granny? Beats me.

There are Brighton branches of Hotel Chocolat and Montezuma's but the real rising star in this neighbourhood is a bean-to-bar maker in Hassocks, a large village a few miles outside the town, working, in the time-honoured British eccentric manner, in a shed at the bottom of his garden.

Actually, it is more of a cabin than a shed, and James Hull is too serious to be considered eccentric. But it is fair to say that he is still some way from being a household name.

James caught the chocolate bug at a food demonstration where the chef was explaining the various ways in which chocolate can be flavoured. At the end of the demo there was time for questions, and someone in the audience – someone with a first-rate mind, in my view – asked the chef how she made her chocolate.

With commendable honesty, the chef confessed that she bought it in ready-made and then melted it down, as countless high street 'luxury' 'artisan' chocolatiers also do.

> " James caught the chocolate bug at a food demonstration where the chef was explaining the various ways in which chocolate can be flavoured

But James Hull is a questing, curious soul, and he got to pondering about the whole business of how chocolate came into being, and dug around for more information.

"I was wondering," James recalled, "how many companies that sell chocolates in this country actually make their own chocolate, and if they don't, then why not? I was surprised to find in the UK that we only had a couple of actual chocolate makers, and one of those was Cadbury..."

It's a nasty moment of truth, and many of us have endured the same painful process of discovery. Not so many of us, though, have set off single-mindedly to do something about it. James did, though he deprecates his initial efforts.

"I gathered information from old books, and from the internet," he told me. "And, a little stupidly, I thought, 'Well, how hard can it be?'"

James's first port of call was the London Chocolate Show at Olympia, where he picked the brains of Britain's little band of bean-to-bar makers, and managed to source a couple of kilograms of Nicaraguan beans.

Thus armed, he set about making his own chocolate from scratch. James was Living the Dream, and he remembers every detail of those first experiments.

"I roasted the beans in the oven," he said, "cooled them with a desk fan, cracked them with a rolling pin, de-shelled them individually by hand, winnowed them with a hairdryer, and lastly stuck them in a blender to become chocolate."

Sadly, however, not all went according to plan. "After blowing up two blenders and only managing to produce a very gritty paste, it quickly became apparent that producing chocolate from scratch was no easy feat."

But they build them tough in Hassocks, West Sussex, and James was not going to let a couple of relatively minor explosions deter him from his chosen path. He had read that old-fashioned chocolate factories used to employ large stone grinders called *mélangeurs* to refine their roasted beans into what was essentially smooth liquid chocolate.

A large stone grinder was both out of James's price range and incompatible with the dimensions of his hut (sorry, cabin), but after a bit of lateral thinking and some poking around on Amazon he came up with a diminutive Indian spice grinder that he reckoned would do the same sort of job, but on a smaller scale.

And he was right. "It was definitely not what the spice grinder was designed for," he reflected. "And quite possibly not what it should be used for. But it worked perfectly. I had created chocolate!"

What had begun as a hobby quickly gathered pace. Family, then friends, were called into action as enthusiastic tasters, and soon test bars were being passed around to friends of friends, and from all came the same response with increasing volume and frequency: "Why don't you put this stuff on the market?"

And so, in August 2015, J Cocoa was launched. The feedback, from the public and from competition judges, was every bit as enthusiastic as that of James's family and friends. His single-origin, bean-to-bar beauties sold well right from the start, and word of mouth soon brought him a reliable customer base and the resources to invest in some slightly more substantial equipment – and to broaden the range of beans that he uses.

But he hasn't lost sight of his principles. Of course he wants to make tasty chocolate, but James also has ambitions to use his business as "an avenue to implement real change in cocoa-growing countries", which, he rightly points out, are often in the poorest of the planet's regions, and which have an unfortunate record of past exploitation.

Not only that, but: "I have always personally been concerned for our environment and realise that I need to be environmentally conscious with the business in conjunction with trying to bring about lasting economic change." Since, he pointed out, there is not much point in bringing about lasting economic change if in the process you reduce the planet to an uninhabitable garbage heap. So J Cocoa generates the minimum possible quantities of waste and pollution. "After all," James said, "this is the only planet with chocolate on it!"

James's particular part of the planet, Hassocks, is well worth a visit if you are in that neck of the woods, although at present the small scale of the J Cocoa operation precludes public involvement.

The village has the unusual distinction of being named after its railway station, rather than the other way round. The story goes that when the Southern Railway were extending their line from London in this direction in the first half of the 19th century, they got to the neighbouring parishes of Clayton and Keymer and decided that the two should share a station.

What, the railway company asked the two communities, should the station be called? Naturally, declared the inhabitants of Clayton, it should be called 'Clayton'. No, no! cried the Keymerites, it is as plain as the nose on your face that the station must be named 'Keymer'.

Agreement could not be reached, and just when pitchforks were being sharpened on either side, a railwayman with a gift for diplomacy noticed a farm on the road to nearby Hurstpierpoint named Hassocks Gate. We shall call our new station Hassocks, he declared, and that was that.

The eventual effect of all the bickering was that both Clayton and Keymer fell from public attention into virtual obscurity, while the greater whole known as Hassocks acquired five churches, four pubs and the fame that goes with a regular mention in the Departures announcements at Victoria Station.

A good tale to tell your travelling companions while enjoying a drink in one of those four pubs. Do raise a glass to James Hull while you are there – he'll be in his shed just up the way, making beautiful chocolate.

His latest projects include a vegan salted caramel, at the suggestion – or it might have been the insistence – of his girlfriend, who is that way inclined, and which she deems so successful that she has suggested that James should now turn his entire range vegan. He has pointed out, he told me, that Solkiki already do that kind of thing very well. We await developments.

One more innovation in the J Cocoa pipeline is a collaboration with the oil and vinegar purveyors Stratta, who James met at a food market.

"They had a chocolate balsamic vinegar which they were flavouring with cocoa powder, so I suggested they try out some cocoa nibs that I would roast for them and see if it made a better flavour," James said. "Wow, did it! The flavour really transferred — it was incredible, and the chocolate balsamic vinegar is truly a beautiful creation." One that James is now selling on a small scale, and working to see if it can be scaled up for a larger production run.

There are two reasons to love the story of this collaboration: one is that it perfectly illustrates the questing mind and collaborative spirit of the bean-to-bar maker; and the other is that it brings us a step closer to the wonderful goal of a chocolate salad.

> " The flavour really transferred — it was incredible, and the chocolate balsamic vinegar is truly a beautiful creation

If a brief passage through Hassocks has left you ravenous for a quality chocolate snack, head for nearby Brighton. Here I suggest that, unless you are cake-crazy, you choose Montezuma's. There are branches elsewhere, but Montezuma's spiritual home is here.

Rather like Chococo, Montezuma's was founded (in Brighton) by a husband-and-wife team, and pays careful attention to the sourcing of its raw materials.

But where Chococo concentrates mostly on filled chocolates and sells in its own shops/cafes, Montezuma's makes mostly bars and sells in shops — both its own and many others.

The Brighton branch — no longer at the original location, but close — is handy for the Instagram-friendly Brighton Pavilion, if you are a fan of insane heritage architecture and/or loopy royalty, and the Theatre Royal, if your cultural tastes are marginally more mainstream.

I always find Brighton good in parts, like a big bar of so-so chocolate studded with seriously delicious nuts and fruit. There are little corners of great delight and beauty, and clusters of extreme joy (what is the Pavilion if not a cluster of nuttiness?) but also great swathes of average modern dullness.

But it is without question Britain's greatest urban concentration of green-ness and gayness, and a suitable spot for the foundation of a company that trumpets its ethical credentials and loves to dress up its products in glorious pastel shades.

Montezuma's founders are Helen and Simon Pattinson, who met as young lawyers keen to travel the world. Leaving their jobs behind, they set out for South America, where one night they camped on a cacao plantation, ate plenty of the chocolate that grew there, and came up with a wild and crazy notion for their future together.

When they got back to the UK they set up in a lovely little shop in Brighton, hand-making all their chocolate products themselves, using ethically sourced raw materials, of course.

As the business grew, so did their family. Three little girls arrived as more shops and more staff were added to their developing empire.

Helen and Simon kept the promise they had made to themselves to do things the right way as the business continued to expand. They started regular support of a charity based in Chichester called Children on the Edge, which supports young people in many locations who are on the verge of destitution.

Montezuma's shops are lively, and so are the flavours of the bars. Some might find them a bit clunky, hefty in aspect and forthright in flavour, but to me they are a reliable standby for a long journey, and I have always found the shop staff enthusiastic and helpful.

These days Montezuma's is really quite substantial, in terms of scale somewhere between Chococo and Hotel Chocolat. There are production facilities near Chichester, a little group of shops of their own, and significant export agreements with others overseas, including the United States. There are 150 or so staff and the company's annual turnover has been reported to be in the region of £10 million a year.

Helen and Simon recently sold a majority stake in the business to a Scottish firm of private equity investors, but have stayed on to run their brainchild. In a sense, Montezuma's is drifting beyond the remit of this book, but I like the shops and I believe that the founders remain committed to the principles with which they set out.

"The ideals we started out with have stayed with us and are firmly rooted," Helen has declared. It's an important statement. Not all of the chocolate makers in this book dream of becoming millionaires or achieving global domination. Some of them just want to make good chocolate, and enough money to feed their families.

> Not all of the chocolate-makers in this book dream of becoming millionaires or achieving global domination. Some of them just want to make good chocolate, and enough money to feed their families

But there is nothing inherently wrong with being successful. Little chocolate companies that become big companies create lots of experienced chocolate makers and chocolate advocates en route.

And substantial chocolate companies have the opportunity to do a substantial amount of good with the communities whose crops they buy. Willie Harcourt-Cooze has done more to ensure sustainable prosperity for the Venezuelans with whom he works than their rotten government has achieved in a decade. Angus Thirlwell and Hotel Chocolat have thoroughly revitalised the growing of cacao on St Lucia, where it was in danger of becoming lost to future generations.

One or two hardcore chocolate fans of my acquaintance expressed concern when Hotel Chocolat obtained a stock market listing, and then again when Montezuma's sold a majority stake to private equity investors.

But each of these decisions was taken by the people who founded the organisations involved. The deals were, in a very real sense, their business. And one has to hope that investors who have put money into such deals recognise that they became successful by operating in a principled manner, and can become more successful by continuing to operate that way.

That is the way that Helen Pattinson sees the future, at least for now. "As a small family business we try pretty damn hard to ensure we do a good job with equity and integrity," she said.

"In the end what matters is that we produce a great product and we do it in a way that makes sense in the long term. We changed our direction in life because we wanted something different and we are striving towards a business that can also offer something different to our partners."

As long as they offer decent chocolate to us in the meantime, that is fine by me.

Montezuma's: Loads of ethically sourced bars. I like the dark with orange and geranium (about £2.60, ocado. com). They make reliably good bags of buttons, both flavoured and unflavoured, and plenty of child-friendly yet relatively low-sugar creations. The (high cocoa) milk chocolate buttons have proved a great hit with young chocolate fans.

TASTING NOTES

J Cocoa: James Hull's range depends, as it should, on what top-quality beans he has most recently been able to source, but I have recently enjoyed a terrific 70% Rugoso dark and a gentle 30% Chuno milk. If you know of anyone unfortunate enough to suffer from a Galaxy habit, you could wean them off the muck with James's Chuno milk. They'll thank you for it one day.

Winchester Fine Chocolates: Zara Snell is really going from strength to strength and her winter spice almost makes shivering in the sleet worthwhile. It is "A spiced raspberry milk chocolate truffle with merlot-infused salt, encased within a milk chocolate shell." Zara's latest brainchild, brought to market just as I finished writing this chapter, is a honey truffle made with the golden deliciousness of locally sourced Three Hares Honey, encased in 66% dark *couverture* from the respectable continental specialists Valrhona. Ohhh...

☐ **Winchester Cocoa Company:** I really enjoyed meeting Chris Attewell at the Chocolate Show in London recently, and he is always keen to talk to fans. Watch out for his pop-up shop in Winchester in the run-up to Christmas – a cup of delicious single-origin hot chocolate is highly recommended – or get in touch online to buy his brilliant soft centres and bars.

☐ **Chococo Winchester:** So many lovely things. See the Tasting Notes for Chococo in the Dorset chapter.

WALES

THE HILLS ARE ALIVE

USEFUL INFO

NomNom I am the last person on the planet you should ask for directions to the Abandoned Chocolate Factory, since I totally failed to find it when equipped with the finest technology I could lay my mitts on.

No matter. Go to the NomNom website (**nomnom. cymru**) for the latest news on building and/or refurbishment plans. Who knows? It might all be coming together – I hope so. And at least you will be able to order the chocolate, which is gorgeous. NomNom bars are also available from the tremendous Gloucestershire services on the M5 (both directions) and at branches of Sourced Market.

Forever Cacao Pablo is a lovely man and made me tremendously welcome but he works from the family home and they are not geared up for public visits. Instead I suggest that you check out his website, **forevercacao.co.uk**, or, if you are in North Wales or thereabouts, some of the shops and cafes that stock his bars.

These are Pablo's recommendations:

Cultivate

**Glanhafren Market Hall
26 Market Street**

Newtown SY16 2PD

cultivate.uk.com

07498 756148

Open: Tue–Sat 9am–5pm

This food shop is a social enterprise linking local growers and makers with the community.

Dyfi Wholefoods

40 Heol Maengwyn

Machynlleth SY20 8EB

01654 700552

Open: Mon–Sat 9am–5.30pm

Just across the border back in England:

Honeysuckle Wholefoods
53 Church Street
Oswestry SY11 2SZ
01691 653125

Herbarium
21 Wyle Cop
Shrewsbury SY1 1XB
Open: Mon–Sat 9.30am–5pm

Chocolate Gourmet
16 Castle Street
Ludlow SY8 1AT
chocolategourmet.co.uk
Open: Mon–Fri 10am–5pm; Sat 10am–5.30pm;
Sun 11am–4pm

Heist Mikey has been busy networking, and there
is a long list of stockists (with clickable links) at
heistchocolate.com/stockists

Among them I'd recommend **Wright's Food
Emporium (Golden Grove Arms, Llanarthne SA32
8JU)**, a cafe/provisions/wineshop: Mon 11am–5pm;
Tue closed; Wed–Thu 11am–7pm; Fri–Sat 9am–
late (last supper orders 9pm); Sun 11am–5pm
wrightsfood.co.uk/#cheerful

THE LOST FACTORY

When I am not travelling the land to seek out new and exciting forms of chocolate, I work in a busy newspaper office where my colleagues are delighted to help me assess any discoveries.

Over the last few years they may have become weary of the chore, but to their credit I have never heard them complain. It could be that when my back is turned this crack squad of lifestyle experts turn to each other and moan about the sheer volume of top-quality chocolate they are forced to consume in the name of research, but they are kind and polite enough to disguise any such feelings of boredom and satiation from me.

In fact, their responses are almost unfailingly enthusiastic and I have been able to compile a mental hit parade of which makers and flavours they most enjoy, so that if deadlines and editorial whims have been weighing heavily upon us I can produce a beloved bar to raise the spirits.

Nothing produces elation among my colleagues so rapidly and profoundly as NomNom's peanut butter bar, a confection that I hold to be – after exhaustive research dedicated to this question alone – the most moreish bar of chocolate in the world.

It is not a grand item. Concept and presentation are straightforward. The chocolate is good (Venezuelan); the peanuts crushed sufficiently to be integrated but not lost. There is salt, but not too much. It is coherent. It is unutterably delicious.

The bar is simply foiled, and wrapped in brown paper with its name spelled out in black type. The company's name is hardly pretentious or classy. It's the noise that the makers want people to make when they unwrap their bars (or see them, or just think about them, as I am now): NomNom.

I found NomNom's bars at an upmarket deli around the corner from the office, and once we had worked our way through half a dozen or so of the peanut butter bars (just to make sure that we had not been suffering a mass olfactory hallucination) we checked out, comprehensively, the rest of the range: chilli, marmalade, coffee, and a brilliant white chocolate and pistachio number that is pale green and speckly, melts on your fingers and slips down a treat.

None of the bars were immaculate: they could be a little messy in appearance, and the wrapping wasn't always neat (a sure sign that it was being performed by hand, and not by machine) but there was an exuberance about the recipes and their execution that was incredibly endearing, and when I looked a little more into the company's background, another, unexpected element was added into the mix: a sense of mystery.

The bars were made, according to the wrappers, at The Abandoned Chocolate Factory in Llanboidy, somewhere in the hills above Carmarthen in Wales. What was all that about?

The NomNom website told of a factory that for 25 years had belonged to Pemberton's Chocolate, an old-school family firm that occupied former agricultural premises for two decades and prospered, winning international fame and once making the chocolate statuettes presented to diners at the Oscars ceremony. But a decade ago it closed down, and remained abandoned, with much of its kit gathering dust.

Until, the story goes, it was rediscovered by Liam Burgess, who in 2017 launched an ambitious plan to restore production to the abandoned premises.

Liam had grown up over the road from the factory, and visited for a tour when he was 10. Apart from an apparently world-famous tug-of-war team, the chocolate factory was the most famous thing about Llanboidy, and when he grew up and started making chocolates of his own in a nearby former cowshed, the old factory remained in Liam's mind.

So eventually he and his small team moved into the semi-derelict premises. "We were just a bunch of kids, making chocolate bars in a cowshed. How are we ever going to move into this massive, giant chocolate factory? But... we did."

And when they did, according to a charming video interview with Liam on the NomNom website, they discovered an amazing treasure trove of chocolate moulds. "Thousands of them – 4,132, to be exact." In all kinds of shapes, for all the seasonal and celebratory items that Pemberton's used to produce: "Ducks, bunnies, pigs, penguins, cockerels, chickens... it's all here."

Liam's plan was to get chocolate enthusiasts involved in the restoration of the old factory. Via the website, he invited people to come along, buy a mould and decorate it as the mood took them, before carrying it away as a memento and piece of folk art.

One day soon, he hoped that the leaks in the roof would be repaired, and the dilapidated premises would once again echo to the happy noise of young people joyfully making chocolate. From the video it is clear that it happened, at least in part and at least for a while.

But the page of the website where the curious may book group tours of the factory says "Opening hours to be posted soon" and has said that for quite some time now…

I am a romantic about chocolate – I love to believe in poetic tales of forest origins and indigenous growers, of ancestral harvesting techniques… and of atmospheric artisanal processing places, of bare brick and sputtering bulbs, creaking machinery and a tough, close-knit team doing their best against the odds.

> " I am a romantic about chocolate – I love to believe in poetic tales of forest origins and indigenous growers, of ancestral harvesting techniques…

I am also a journalist, and I love a mystery, a quest, a journey into the unknown. The search for NomNom promised all of that.

But it didn't quite deliver, and that may well be my fault.

I emailed NomNom. I telephoned. No response to the emails. No answer on the phone (and no answerphone). I asked people who had worked with NomNom a few months before if they could tell me how to get in touch.

I did all of the above several times, to no avail. In the end I just got in the car and drove to Llanboidy. I thought: "It's a factory. How hard can it be to find a factory?"

Quite hard. West on the M4, over the Severn and into Wales and further on, until the M4 ceases to be, on the fringes of Pontarddulais, then up into the gentle hills towards, and beyond, Carmarthen. Sarnau, Bancyfelin, and further still, along roads which narrow and tighten, and often share their route with streams. Old finger signposts indicate villages which turn out to be barely hamlets, and then farmsteads, and then nothing at all.

Amazing. Not so long after my failure to find Willie's chocolate factory in the Blackdown Hills, I had failed to find another one in the foothills of the Black Mountains.

Where the chocolate factory should have been was a crossroads between farm tracks. I trundled down the first, at great hazard to the Golf's undercarriage. At the entrance to the yard at the end, damp stone and stable doors secured by string, stood a man of indeterminate age, whose damp black coat was also secured by string. Next to him stood an elderly sheepdog.

He looked curious to see me. I wound down the window.

"Is there a chocolate factory hereabouts?"

He shook his head, seemed to have a second thought, looked down at the dog as if for confirmation. Shook his head again.

"Okay!" I said, cheerily. A mistake anyone could make, I meant my tone to suggest. "I'll just turn round, then."

The man nodded.

Back at the crossroads, over the 'main' road, and down another farm track – which was, I now noticed, in considerably better shape than the first. A better bet all round. At the end of this driveway, after several speed humps, was a much more handsome farmyard, flanked by well-tended buildings. Quite empty, though.

I hopped out of the car and looked around a corner. And there in plain sight was a set of medieval-style stocks, such as the local populace might employ to secure unpopular folk in order to pelt them with vegetables.

Stocks of recent manufacture, I noted with mounting unease, the hefty, hinged assembly painted shiny back, and boasting a steel padlock and chain for greater security. Blimey, I thought, whoever gets put in that is not getting out in a hurry… And then it occurred to me that getting out in a hurry was a tremendously good idea, and I was back in the Golf and yomping over the speed bumps before you could say 'involuntary incarceration'.

That rather took the steam out of my efforts. I gave up on the satnav and tried Google Maps, with similarly unsuccessful results. I asked a young lady walking two sheepdogs if she knew of… but she didn't. It was getting dark. It was drizzling. I decided to head north, in search of Llansantffraid, and Forever Cacao.

Somewhere in the gathering gloom around me, I was confident, people were making messy but delicious chocolate bars. One day, perhaps, I would find them. But it wouldn't be today.

The most vociferous fans of bean-to-bar chocolate insist that something of the *terroir* is expressed in the finished chocolate: a term taken from wine connoisseurship which suggests that in a bar one can taste, or at least detect, a sense of the land, the territory, on which the beans were grown.

Hotel Chocolat have tested this with bars made not only from their own plantation but from a single side (they borrow, cheekily, the French term *côte*) of that estate, which Angus Thirlwell of HC insists taste entirely distinctive from chocolate made with beans grown elsewhere on the island of St Lucia.

I'm not so sure about that. But there is something very distinctive about all the bars made at the top of a windy hill in North Wales. It may be that the bean-to-bar bars made by Forever Cacao owe much of their flavour to the spot on which the beans that make the chocolate are grown – a spot known only to the Ashaninka people of Peru who grow them.

It may be that the flavours are at least in part attributable to the fact that the beans are 'raw' or unroasted.

But I think that a great deal of the distinctiveness of a bar of Forever Cacao chocolate can be ascribed to the place in which the beans are ground and the chocolate is made, and the spirit in which the processes take place. Up on this hill is Pablo Spaull's country. This is his *terroir*.

"I'm at home here," Pablo told me as we sat with cups of tea in his low-beamed kitchen.

"Well, clearly," I said. "This is where you live."

"I mean that I've always been at home here. I've always lived around here. There's a pillar on top of one of these hills — Rodney's Pillar — and I've never lived out of sight of that pillar. The last three houses I have lived in, going back a good few years now, have all been on this same ridge of hills. Something's going on there. Some kind of energy is at work."

I am no sort of a hippy and not even an apprentice mystic, but on the morning that I visit I can sense the energy that he is talking about. A powerful and beneficent sense of place.

These borderlands are thoroughly peculiar. When I was driving over to Llansantffraid that morning I had been chasing showers across the Marcher lands on the Welsh borders, and through the strange sandstone settlement of Ruyton XI Towns. Please indulge a short digression on this extraordinary place. It is ancient, of Anglo-Saxon origins and constructed largely in the local stone in the most striking manner, but the remarkable thing about it is the name: not a reference to the Chinese premier, but the only Roman numerals in any British placename, and referring to the 11 townships of which the (now ruined) castle had charge. The settlements are Coton, Eardiston, Felton, Haughton, Rednal, Ruyton itself, Shelvock, Shotatton, Sutton, Tedsmore and Wykey. Arthur Conan Doyle, who would go on to create Sherlock Holmes, worked in Ruyton for a short while as a medical student in 1878; later he would refer to the town dismissively as "not big enough to make one town, far less eleven". But I thought it was a lovely little place. And one of the 11 towns surely inspired Shelvock Holmes.

As I drove out of the far side of Ruyton there was a rainbow sitting in the distance among the first of the hills of Wales, and I thought to myself, "There's chocolate

> **"** I am no sort of a hippy and not even an apprentice mystic, but on the morning that I visit I can sense the energy that he is talking about. A powerful and beneficent sense of place

in them thar hills," and then when I finally got to Pablo's village and rang him up and got the directions and chugged all the way up the hill, there was the rainbow, a little tiny rainbow, sitting on Pablo's forehead. Good grief, I thought, is there something in the air up here...?

There was a crystal ball – just a tiny faceted globe, hanging in the kitchen window and catching the sun that streamed in, and from time to time as we spoke it cast a rainbow across his temple... Pull yourself together, I told myself.

Pablo's house sits almost on top of a steep green hill with the village of Llansantffraid far below and a row of similar peaks marching into the distance. We are only 10 miles from the border with England, and perhaps 50 from Birmingham, but the scenery is distinctively Welsh, wild and elemental, and a fresh, crisp breeze blows on top of the hill that suggests that weather arrives up here with great speed and little warning.

But it is a good spot for a house, and a productive spot for a farm. These hills give good grazing, and the same thought must have occurred to whoever built the house here in the first place, many hundreds of years ago.

The heart of the building is a 'cruck' house, built around vast curved timbers. Which may, in this case, be Spanish in origin. Hang on, Pablo. They may be what?

"At Porthmadog they broke up ships that ran aground from the Spanish Armada, or so they say. The word is, these timbers came from one of those."

It is just about feasible, looking at the curving pillars of wood, to think of that as their origin. Tempting, too.

That's one of the stories that Pablo heard in this house as a youngster, when he visited for parties as a teenager. Years later, when the house came onto the market, he returned to have a look – and remembered that he had been here before and loved it.

It just felt like the right place to be, he reckons. The house called to him in the same way that chocolate first did, at another party.

> **"It was a friend's 40th birthday, and I was DJ-ing,"** Pablo says. "Someone there had this raw chocolate and I ate a whole slab and just felt this incredible energy. It kept me going all night…

"It was a friend's 40th birthday, and I was DJ-ing," Pablo says. "Someone there had this raw chocolate and I ate a whole slab and just felt this incredible energy. It kept me going all night…"

That kicked him off on a search for the raw energy that he had felt, a search that led not only to a vegan diet but also to the work that his friend Dilwyn Jenkins, author of the *Rough Guide to Peru*, had been doing with the Ashaninka tribe.

Dilwyn, who sadly died five years ago, was a figure of great significance and inspiration to those dedicated to what used to be known as 'alternative lifestyles' – a holistic approach to living that is respectful of the planet and of the rights and traditions of indigenous peoples.

These philosophies have been deeply rooted in the wilder areas of Wales for decades now – thanks in no small part to the work of Dilwyn Jenkins. But he also did amazing things in Peru, working with the Ashaninka to export the coffee that the tribe grows and find markets for it overseas. It was a natural progression to do the same job for the cacao that grows naturally alongside the coffee. Which is where Pablo came in.

The farming of the trees is naturally organic, as the tribe have never used pesticides or chemicals of any kind and are not about to start doing so now.

The purity of the crop and the 'close to the land' profile of the people who grow it all feed into the near-mystical regard that Pablo has for his ingredients. Which makes it all the more refreshing that the magic that transforms beans into chocolate happens not in a smoke-filled shamanic hut on the top of his private mountain, but in a repurposed shipping container parked next to the house.

Not just any old shipping container, mind you. It has a history. "This container used to be the services office at the Glastonbury Festival," Pablo proudly announced, turning down the music blaring from the radio that had been accompanying his work prior to my arrival. "I heard that it was looking for another home – and it just seems right, really."

It's worth pointing out at once that, while talk of festivals, energies and forces crops up often in conversation with Pablo, and while he is a former DJ who still hits the decks on a regular basis, he's an easy-going, warm and funny man with a good line in self-deprecation and full awareness of the way that the world works.

What he's doing up here is not self-indulgence: he has two children to care for (his son was off up the hill with his wife and the dog; his daughter was pottering around upstairs) and a beautiful old house to run.

So Pablo is well versed in the realities of life. He just has very firm views about how his life should be led.

Some things are not to be compromised. The cleanliness of the chocolate kitchen is exemplary (the hygiene certificate sits on top of the order forms next to the laptop) and is matched by the domestic kitchen next door.

The beans, which arrive from Peru in fat sacks, are in prime condition, due to the work of those who grow them, but also due to the hard work that Pablo and the late Dilwyn have put in with the Ashaninka to improve their knowledge of bean preparation.

And the processes – in the conching shed and the kitchen – are quality controlled by Pablo to a degree that almost no other chocolate maker can match.

"I know that it is all being done in exactly the right way," Pablo said. "Because I am the one doing it all."

All of it? Even the fiddly and – let's face it – fairly boring business of wrapping the bars when they are ready to go to market?

"All of it. The children might get to stick the stickers on the wrappers when I'm done. If they're lucky…"

Utterly professional. But Pablo is not wedded to the capitalist goals of expansion and profit margins. He works hard, but he knows where his priorities lie. "I want to be around the children when they are growing up, really spend time with them," he said. "They won't be at home for ever, and I don't want to miss any of it."

When he was starting out, a man from the Welsh Development Agency came to visit, with kindly intent. He sat at the kitchen table and waved spreadsheets and projections at Pablo, prodded a laptop and said that Forever Cacao would need to do this, that and the other in order to succeed.

"He said, 'You'll have to be turning over this much in six months or you'll have no chance of surviving as a business,'" Pablo recalled. And it was clear that grants from the agency would be tied to doing things their way, at least as far as agreeing business targets. Pablo said thanks, but no thanks. "It's just not the way that I want to operate."

The same goes for marketing, which is gentle, and largely by word of mouth, and for distribution – ditto. "I've turned down one or two places who wanted to stock the bars," Pablo said, with a suggestion of regret. "I don't want to upset people, but I'd seen the other things that they were selling, and I just don't think that our bars fit in with that."

Remember that Pablo first came across the wonders of raw chocolate by consuming an entire hefty bar of the stuff, so the question of energy, in the way that the bar is made, and in the atmosphere and locations in which it is sold, is of paramount importance. That is also why he uses raw cacao, unroasted beans, in his work.

The Ashaninka use cacao in ceremonies, in the same way that South and Central American communities have for centuries. Cadbury, in the plodding dioramas at their 'world' in Bournville, try to appropriate these traditions in order to legitimise the sugar- and fat-laden goop that they inflict on the world.

Pablo tries to keep his bars closer to their origin in a much more basic way, by dispensing with the processes that industrialisation places between bean and consumer. Which includes doing away with the process that is central to almost all chocolate manufacture on every scale: the roasting of the bean.

"I just feel that you get more of the vibe in the natural state," Pablo said, handing me a chunk of a bar, studded with cacao nibs, that he had finished in the work kitchen six feet away from where we sat at his family table.

It was beautiful: sharp, strong flavours, and textural crunch from the nibs. "These bars are made with special beans," Pablo emphasised. "They come from the Ashaninka and I want to preserve what comes from them, not lose it. Of course I've tried roasting them, but you lose that fruitiness, that fizzle and sparkle that I love."

As I listened to Pablo enthuse I was savouring the flavours of his bar, which reminded me that alongside the passionate commitment to his family and his ideals, Pablo also has great determination to make damn fine chocolate, applying skills that he learned, soon after his first encounter with the raw chocolate bar, by seeking out the expertise of those who might be regarded as the tribal elders of bean-to-bar chocolate making.

"I learned from Willie [Harcourt-Cooze]," Pablo said. "And from Ali [Gower] at Chocolate Tree in Edinburgh, and of course from Duffy [Sheardown]. Bean to bar, it's all about Willie and Ali and Duffy, isn't it?" These days there are more than just this semi-legendary triumvirate, but Pablo certainly went to the right people when he was seeking knowledge.

"I called up Duffy and said, 'Can I come and see you?'" Pablo recalled. "He said 'Sure' and I got there and there were all these amazing machines and I said, 'Can you teach me how to do it?' And he said, 'I can tell you – I can tell you what the machines are and which button to press, but I can't teach you...'"

Some things, I reckon Duffy meant, you can only learn by doing. And making bean-to-bar chocolate is about so much more than pressing the right button. It is about a deep understanding of your materials, and how they change, and what causes them to change. It takes time, and dedication, and patience.

But surviving as an independent chocolate maker also requires a certain amount of business sense, because high ideals, as my late grandmother was fond of saying, butter no parsnips. There is not much point making beautiful chocolate with the beans of the Ashaninka people if none of the people of Britain want to buy them.

On this point, as on others, Pablo sought the advice of the elders. He asked Duffy Sheardown, who has made a great and international success of his chocolate business from a shed in Cleethorpes, how one might judge if an area might support an independent chocolate business. Duffy suggested that Pablo should visit the local breweries and bakers.

"Duffy told me, 'If your area can support a micro-brewery and a proper bakery, then it can support someone making chocolate in the right way.'"

And so it has. And as the community around Llansantffraid has supported Pablo's business, so has the wider bean-to-bar community. "That's the way it has been," Pablo confirmed. "Among the bar makers, there's no need to compete with each other, we're really not stealing each other's business. There are enough people around who like good chocolate and understand the way that we do things to keep us all in business."

I have been to many a gathering of artisan makers at fairs and festivals and award ceremonies and the like and can confirm that this is true. Of course, chocolate makers compare notes with each other, especially when two or more of them have taken different approaches with similar beans but, as Pablo put it, "No one is having a go at each other…"

This gentle, funny man is not enthused by competition. But he will admit that, when he first set foot upon his property as an adult, his eyes lit up for a moment with the possibilities.

"When I first saw this farmyard and the buildings in it I thought, OK, I'll have a visitor centre there, and a cafe over there, and we'll park the cars there…," he said, gesturing in the appropriate directions. "And then after a while I thought, 'Hang on, this just isn't the way that I want to do things. I don't want people all over the place, and streams of cars coming up the hill. I don't really want lots of people working for me to make all this happen.'"

Pablo just wants to keep it simple. "I want to do this in a way that works for me and for the family," he said. "I work in batches. In between I can be with the children. That way, the ethos seems right. And if it seems right, I do it, and if it doesn't seem right, I don't…"

Somewhere between the wonderful, grand-scale dreams of NomNom and the chilled, spiritual purity of Forever Cacao lies Heist Chocolate, the Principality's latest chocolate maker.

That's between the two in philosophical terms, not in any geographical sense, because Heist is based in Cardiff, far to the south of Pablo's set-up and a good way east of wherever NomNom might actually be.

It is also an urban set-up rather than a rural one, because Mikey Lewis's one-man operation is located not atop a windy hill or among picturesque hamlets but in a studio space at Meanwhile House, a trendily revamped 1960s office building on the Curran Embankment a few minutes from Cardiff Central Station.

Mikey, a curly-mopped, bespectacled sort, has been making micro-batch bean-to-bar chocolate for a couple of years, and moved into Meanwhile House as a step up from making chocolate at home.

It is, at present, the ultimate small business. "Every bar of Heist chocolate is designed, roasted, ground, tempered, wrapped, stamped and stitched by me," says Mikey.

He is also, he likes to point out, completely self-funded, which together with his minimal staff, goes some way to explaining the stylish packaging – labels designed by local artists and designers, attached to Jiffy envelopes that are hand-sealed by the maker himself.

It is an aesthetic pioneered (with slightly smarter envelopes) by Pump Street in Orford, and highly effective it is too.

The hours are long and the dedication required is extraordinary. But Mikey is on a mission and, like Pablo, seems to have found what he was put on this planet to do. He's building a future, at a rate of 40 bars a day.

☐ **NomNom:** My favourite of theirs, and one of the most addictive chocolate bars on the planet, in my extensive experience, is the peanut butter bar. The pale green pistachio and white chocolate is gently delicious, and the marmalade bar is great, if epically messy.

☐ **Forever Cacao:** My favourite among Pablo's bars, all made with Ashaninka cacao from Peru, is the classic 72% dark. There's a version of the same bar infused with orange which I also love. Remember that Pablo works with raw, unroasted cacao beans.

TASTING NOTES

☐ **Heist:** All of Mikey's bars are £6. I really enjoyed the homely vanilla milk and the orange marmalade, but the classic Madagascan is a better measure of his skills as a bean-to-bar maker, which are impressive. This lad will go far…

HOW TO BE
A CHOCOLATE JUDGE

If you have enjoyed your adventures in tasting fine, single-origin and bean-to-bar chocolate you may like to intensify the process by joining an organised tasting evening, or a masterclass – or by enrolling as a chocolate judge.

Most bean-to-bar and artisan makers offer little chunks of their bars at farmers' markets and chocolate fairs, and that can be a good way to find out more about the comparative flavours of bars from different origins.

Many makers also offer guided tasting evenings, and you can also sign up for tastings and tours with experts such as Sophie Jewett in York, Jennifer Earle (who guides fascinating chocolate tours around London) and Hazel Lee. Up in Scotland, Iain Burnett is developing the notion of a curated 'flight' of chocolates, analogous to the wine flights hosted by distinguished vineyards and wine merchants.

All of these experiences will help you to hone your palate and your tasting skills, and gradually to identify the characteristics of chocolate made using beans from a wide variety of different locations and employing different methods.

The skills and knowledge thus acquired can be taken to their greatest extreme when judging chocolate, either informally among friends or in a more structured way at regional, national and international level.

Judging chocolates can be great fun but often attracts a certain amount of scepticism (not to mention jealousy) among friends and acquaintances.

It can also be very hard work, but at the end of an exhausting day of chocolate-related deliberations I have found sympathy from pals surprisingly hard to come by.

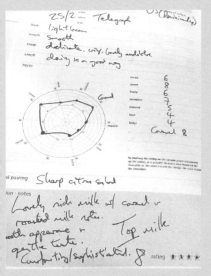

The outcome of all this hard work for the best chocolate makers is the little stickers that you may well see adorning bars of quality chocolate, indicating that the bar has won gold, silver or bronze at an awards ceremony of some great distinction.

The outcome for the judges (unless their constitutions are hardier than mine) is an evening of indigestion and a sleepless night.

Judging chocolate for a major award can involve tasting and comparing as many as 40 different contenders in a session lasting several hours, and it is not only a challenge to the digestive system. A great deal of concentration is required as well.

I have been fortunate to have been asked to judge at the International Chocolate Awards when they were held in London, and every year for the last five I have judged at the British Academy of Chocolate awards, most recently serving on the grand jury which determines who should win gold awards and who should carry off the most prestigious prize of all, the Golden Bean.

The Academy (academyofchocolate.org.uk), which was set up in 2005 by a small group of chocolate professionals, does a great deal more than hand out gongs; it serves as a valuable forum for the chocolate industry and regularly hosts conferences where growers, makers and marketeers from the UK and all over the world can compare notes and discuss the latest important issues. The chair, Sara Jayne Stanes, has been a kind and tremendously valuable source of wisdom and insight for me ever since I started to pursue a serious interest in chocolate.

The Academy's awards, like their international counterparts, are open to chocolate makers from all over the world and receive hundreds of entries in a wide range of categories – not only bars, but filled chocolates, and even hot chocolate and chocolate spreads are lined up for assessment.

The earliest stages of the judging process are a wonderful spectacle, and the logistical challenge alone is enough to boggle the mind, let alone the tastebuds.

Judges sit down at tables arrayed with plates of little chocolate samples, prepared and labelled by a dedicated team of support staff. Each table has a stack of scoresheets at the ready, and slices of apple and unbuttered bread to cleanse the judges' palates between contenders.

Those doing the assessing are a jolly crew of experts, among them food writers, chefs, wine merchants, tour guides and chocolate industry technicians, alongside one or two individuals from quite unrelated walks of life for whom such events are a passionate hobby.

In the early stages, judges sit in groups of half a dozen or so and work their way through categories of entry that have been divided according to type (filled, bar) and then subdivided according to more detailed criteria (bars with inclusions, white chocolate bars, milk chocolate bars, dark chocolate above or below a certain percentage, and so on).

The atmosphere is jovial but also serious; banter is kept to a minimum, gossip frowned upon and speculation about the makers of individual items for tasting is forbidden.

Filled chocolates are sliced into chunks, partly so as not to fill up the judges – but also to allow them to assess the appearance and quality of the fillings. Is that an air bubble? Mark it down. A shell that is too thin, or too substantial? Tut, tut.

Bars are broken into postage-stamp-sized chunks, avoiding as far as conceivably possible any identifying marks. Each sample is tasted by every judge at the table at the same time, to minimise influencing of decisions.

Then the scores are totalled up, and the chocolates which have scored best are referred upwards to a higher jury which will decide if they deserve a medal. Those which have provoked widely varying scores and/or unusually powerful opinions might also be referred on for further consideration.

It's not unusual at the highest level of competition for bean-to-bar chocolate to be judged not only on the straightforward criteria that I outlined in the chapter on tasting (texture, aroma, flavour) but also on the extent to which a bar expresses the characteristics of the area from which it comes. You might have gathered that chocolate from Madagascar often has flavour notes of red fruit — so judges might hope to be able to detect those in a bar made with Madagascan cacao. They might hope for more — to have those notes singing out, or to have them clearly present, but in a complex pattern of other notes.

So when deciding if a bar deserves the highest accolade the judges will be looking for chocolate that is not only made to the very highest standards, but also in its own way distinctive and expressive. Chocolate that speaks of excellence, and announces it in a clear and individual voice.

Once the scores are safely totalled up and the final debates of the grand jury are complete, the identity of the chocolates that have earned accolades are revealed, and judges are free to compare opinions and shower praise on their favourites.

Sandwiches and a glass of something may also be offered at this point, but the judges are unlikely to have much of an appetite.

Multiple samples of chocolate, no matter how good, tend to make the heart race and may even induce a slight queasiness. After judging 40 bars, most of them high-percentage dark, at one competition, I didn't eat or sleep for 24 hours.

A certain amount of mental fatigue is also inevitable, because serious judging requires concentration of the highest order. "Mmm, quite nice," is not a useful reaction; and identifying precisely what one is tasting and then comparing and ranking it in comparison to what one has previously tasted is a challenging business.

But I would recommend the experience to anyone who is interested in developing their knowledge and enjoyment of chocolate among experts. You can't just walk in and sit down as an Academy judge, but they are happy to hear from those with some experience who would be happy to be trained to take part. So have a go...

SCOTLAND

TARTAN TITANS

USEFUL INFO

Chocolate Tree

123 Bruntsfield Place, Edinburgh EH10 4EQ

choctree.co.uk

0131 228 3144

Open: Seven days a week, 10am–7.30pm

Chocolate Tree's shop in Edinburgh is not, strictly speaking, central – but it is no more than a brisk walk from the castle, cathedral, National Gallery and Waverley Station; if you are driving, there are plentiful pay and display parking bays along Bruntsfield Place itself.

CocoaMo Chocolate

As with many artisan chocolatiers, the best way to keep up with Melanie Neil and her latest inventions at CocoaMo is to keep an eye on social media – on Facebook at **facebook.com/ CocoaMochocolates** Her online store at **cocoamochocolates.co.uk** opens twice a year and advance details will be on Facebook.Melanie doesn't have a shop or visitor space at present but anyone with a soul will enjoy the countryside that inspires her work and supplies many of her flavourings andingredients. Helensburgh is a lovely little coastal town, and Loch Lomond and the mountains are just a short way away.

The Highland Chocolatier

Grandtully, Pitlochry PH9 0PL

highlandchocolatier.com

01887 840775

Facebook @IainBurnettTheHighlandChocolatier
Twitter @HighlandChoc

Instagram @IainBurnettChocolatier

Open: Seven days a week 7am–4pm; last orders in the Chocolate Lounge at 3.30pm

Iain Burnett's shop and kitchen in Pitlochry is on the banks of the River Tay in Highland Perthshire, 4 miles from the A9 on the A827. Iain also has the rare distinction among artisan chocolate makers that his shop is individually indicated from main roads: follow the brown tourist road signs marked 'Highland Chocolatier'.

BONNIE BARS
AND BONBONS

The food and drink of Scotland has a worldwide reputation based
on a narrow range of specialities – fabulous fresh fish and game,
haggis (if you must) and, of course, the ubiquitous whisky.

There is a lot of chocolate, too, but much of it is of the spuriously local kind
manufactured – not necessarily in the neighbourhood – by melting down some
bought-in gunk, chucking in some whisky and heather honey and sticking a tartan
wrapper on the result.

All the more important, then, to know where to lay your hands on the real thing.
And the best place to start out on the chocolate trail in Scotland is not far from the
centre of the nation's capital, at the warmly welcoming premises of the Chocolate
Tree, which is not only a cosy cafe stuffed with heartening snacks and wholesome
hot drinks, but also the HQ of Scotland's only bean-to-bar chocolate makers.

It is hugely – and understandably – popular with Edinburgh folk, especially those
local to Bruntsfield Place, a respectable location half a mile from the castle and on
the fringes of the green spaces of Bruntsfield Links and The Meadows, a little off
the main tourist trail but close enough to the centre of the city to feel in touch.

It is a smart but not overwhelmingly genteel area, and there is a lingering sense of
the alternative, which fits in very well with the nurturing and gently countercultural
vibe of Chocolate Tree. Just around the corner, for example, is the original and

largest outpost of the Edinburgh Bicycle Co-operative, the longest established co-op in Scotland.

The Chocolate Tree's roots extend back to 2005, when Alastair and Friederike Gower started to sell carefully sourced and lovingly made organic chocolate around the Scottish alternative festival circuit, operating from portable premises entirely in keeping with their lifestyle and values: a solar-powered geodesic tent.

From festivals the couple graduated to farmers' markets, all the while gradually getting people used to the concept of paying £3.50–£4 for a bar of super-premium organic *couverture* chocolate. "We learned a lot," Ali told me, looking back on those earliest days. "I guess we were trying to educate the customers about what we were doing and why."

That is Ali's typically gentle way of explaining that you can't simply plonk good chocolate down in front of people and expect them to pay a premium for it. You have to explain – with the help of frequent tastings – the amount of time and dedication that goes into each bar, and the intricate processes that result in deep deliciousness. Over a couple of years, Ali and Freddy brought their audience along with them in the enjoyment of carefully crafted organic bars – and then brought in the bean-to-bar concept.

Or, as Ali puts it: "We'd just got them used to paying those sort of prices and enjoying the chocolate and then we said, 'Right, here's something that's twice the price!' and started the education process all over again..."

But the battle for their customers' trust had clearly been won, and Chocolate Tree quickly made new converts with their bean-to-bar products. These are now hardcore fans, who know exactly what they like – and keep coming back for more.

"We've been able to develop a really close relationship with our audience because we have been doing this locally for quite a while now," Ali told me. "And Edinburgh is a great city to be

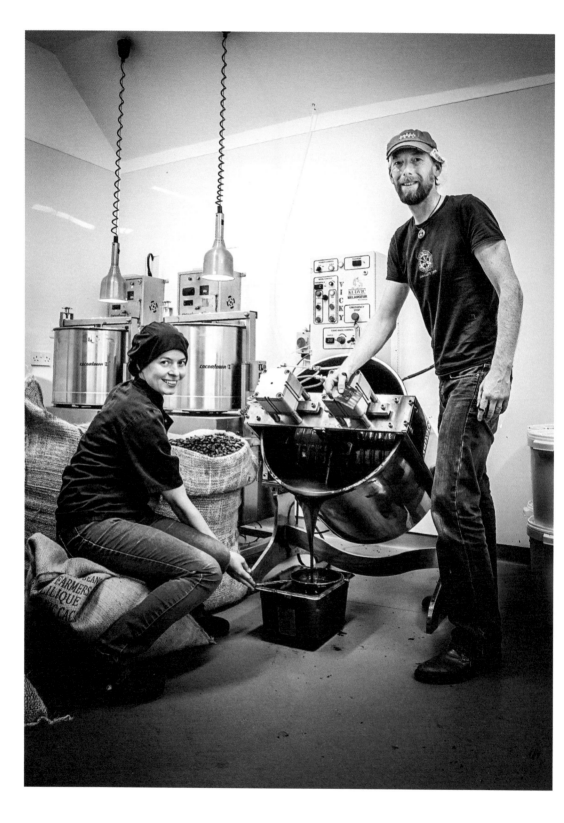

selling chocolate." As noted, the shop is a little way from the centre of town, but it is firmly established in the city's promotional literature and foodie guides, and Edinburgh is a high-profile, world-heritage city that draws tourists – often affluent tourists – from all over the world. It is also a name that customers from overseas who may not be able to travel to Scotland can relate to, and that helps with the brand's profile.

These days, though, Ali and Freddy have recruited a friendly team to run the shop and cafe, meaning that they can spend more time travelling the world looking for new suppliers and ideas, more time in the factory – and more time at home with their children, not far from the production base near Dunbar, 15 miles or so to the east of the capital.

In this commitment to maintaining a rewarding family lifestyle while they develop their business, Ali and Freddy have a lot in common with other artisanal chocolate makers that I encountered elsewhere in Britain – Pablo in North Wales, for example, in his farmhouse on top of the hill with children out walking the dog, and Andy and Claire Burnet in Swanage down on the Jurassic Coast in Dorset.

"Our factory is on a farm near Dunbar, and that allows us the kind of life that we want to live as a family, and to have the kind of business that we want to have," Ali explained. "We are truly passionate about what we do – we have grown the business slowly and organically as we have brought up our family; we are not looking to exit and make big bucks. We really enjoy the process, we have a healthy routine and we get up to healthy activities as a family, Freddy and me and our two children, and I know that there are other chocolate makers who go about their lives in the same way."

I'm not starry-eyed about such a process, and I know how hard it has been for these people to achieve as they have. But I can't help feeling that some of the deep-seated contentment they have found rubs off on what they make. I couldn't tell you what serenity tastes like, but I think there is some of it in a Chocolate Tree bar.

There is an ethical side to all of this as well, which has to do with peace of mind, knowing not only that what do you is in the interests of your family and those who work for you, but also that you have done the right thing in your dealings with those who grow and supply your raw materials.

A common thread among all of the chocolate makers in this book is a concern for ethical dealings with the people who grow cacao. It is easy to imagine, in a rather romantic way, that the best way to do business with a cacao grower must be to visit the plantation or smallholding, negotiate with the farmer a price for a sack of beans that is mutually agreeable, shake hands and head back to the factory to make chocolate.

The reality is different, as Ali explained: it doesn't make economic sense for a maker to incur the huge costs in time and transport involved in visiting a grower; and it doesn't make sense for the grower to waste valuable time greeting, entertaining and negotiating with each individual maker for a small quantity of beans.

Ali knows this, because he has done it. "The one time that we actually went to shake hands at the farm gate, as it were, we ended up losing money on the deal, and I believe the farmer lost money as well."

It might make for a better photo opportunity, but it doesn't make for a sustainable business – for grower or maker.

The solution? "We trade as directly as we can," Ali said. "But really I think the most important thing is to have good partners who have good relationships with the growers and can help them to understand what we need. It's great to go and meet the people involved and we love to do that. But the truth is that we don't have the scale to fill up a container [to go on an ocean-going ship] with beans just for ourselves."

Instead, Chocolate Tree, like other relatively small-scale producers, works with carefully selected, ethically engaged partners, such as Uncommon Cacao and Original Beans, who can work with farmers to ensure high standards of growth and fermentation, and who can buy in sufficient quantities to allow economies of scale in transportation – that is, fill up a container.

But Ali and Freddy still feel that they are on the side of people working on a human scale. "It's good to know that we are working with smallholders," Ali said. "With people who have a couple of hectares and a community of families, all being supported by the way that we're making chocolate."

As for a favourite cocoa-growing region, that's not easy for Ali to choose. "My favourite origin? Wow, that's tricky – there are so many that I love." A bit of thought and a lot of coaxing produces a vote for Mexico: "I love the country, the culture, the cuisine…" But hang on: "They're not actually my favourite beans.

"I love Chililique from Piura in Peru – those beans have the best flavour, they are super-fruity, a little bit like Madagascan." At the Chocolate Tree, they use their bars made with Chililique cacao to 'convert' customers who are new to single-origin bean-to-bar chocolate: "You know, when you get that 'Wow, so that's proper chocolate' moment…"

Ali loves Belize, too. "That's such a wacky place, such a mix ethnographically and demographically, and that really comes through in the cacao…" And of course, Freddy has her own views.

And a vital role in the business. "Being a husband-and-wife team is integral to what we do; we both bring our best to the business," Ali told me. "Freddy designs all our wonderful packaging, and she is a mathematician so she is great at bringing technical input and somehow converting it into works of art."

As well as close family and supplier relationships, there is another bond that helps to keep the Chocolate Tree growing gently and fruitfully. "We still have a really close relationship with our audience," Ali said. "That's so important. Unless you have that contact you are just a brand…"

Heading out of Edinburgh laden down with Chocolate Tree's lovely bars, I had a choice: north into the mountains, or over to the wild west. With half an eye on the forecast (set reasonably fair for Scotland), I shifted my focus to the west coast, and a chocolatier with a passion for her local ingredients, a remarkable background, and an unusual sideline.

You'll have gathered by now that the business of artisanal chocolate making attracts some interesting and forthright characters, and Melanie Neil of CocoaMo chocolate in the little town of Helensburgh certainly ticks those boxes.

CocoaMo is in this book to represent Britain's many individual chocolate makers who work on a small scale in modest premises but do not compromise on taste or quality. I know that there are a good few such makers out there and I would have loved to have included more than space would allow — so look around in your own area and if you hear of an artisan chocolatier operating in the right spirit and the right way on this sort of scale, do give their products a try — you may well unearth a gem, and you are sure to make a friend.

Melanie's background would not immediately suggest a career in fine chocolate. Both her parents were in the emergency services (father a firefighter, mother a nurse), and the first phase of Melanie's professional life followed that kind of an arc, with a decade as an army medic followed by a stint with the NHS in Scotland. She retired from the NHS at the age of 39 to pursue a new path, one that she told me represented "more of a passion than a career change".

She wanted to learn to make top-quality chocolate, and found an excellent tutor in Ruth Hinks, of Cocoa Black chocolate and pastry school in Peebles, Scotland, a former World Chocolate Master with 25 years' experience in the kitchen. The training was pretty intense, but then Melanie is not afraid of hard work – witness not only her military and NHS past, but her 'hobby' of the martial art taekwondo, in which pursuit she is a senior international for Scotland.

With Hinks, she picked up the essential skills of the chocolatier as well as a host of background knowledge about origins, tasting and flavour combinations. At the same time she was mapping out business plans and scoping out her local area for opportunities – and potential competition.

All the indications were positive, and at the end of 2014 she launched CocoaMo. "I knew right from the start what I wanted CocoaMo to be," Melanie told me. "Indulgent, unique and artisan. I didn't want to be lost in, or compared to, all the 'shop-bought' chocolate that was so readily available; I needed to be different, to stand out, for this new venture to work."

Her distinctive tactic was to launch just two collections a year, summer and winter, to allow her to showcase seasonal, local and wild ingredients – and they would only be available online.

The 'soft' launch, trading mainly via friends, word of mouth and online recommendations, was a success, and before Christmas that year Melanie had been invited to showcase her chocolates at four 5-star hotels.

Round about this time she very kindly made contact with me via social media and sent me some of her chocolates to try. They were clearly well made, but I was particularly taken by the wit and invention of their creator, her humour and enthusiasm. I've been a fan ever since, and Melanie is clearly not running out of inspiration. Where does it come from?

"Anywhere!"

Her chocolates always have a story to tell. Last summer's collection was influenced by the concept of afternoon tea, because Melanie had been watching a film about Queen Victoria and was moved to work on a box of suitable bonnie bonbons. The box was labelled 'Afternoon Tea with the High Raj' and the aim was to transport customers back to British Colonial India, where they might be enjoying tea outside on the veranda, looking out onto pristine cut lawns and billowing tea plantations.

Inside the box were bonbons flavoured with wild rose and Scottish raspberry, with Bangladeshi Tetulia tea water, with Earl Grey tea and confit lemon, with chai spice and candied ginger – and there was a mango bonbon named 'The Munshi', who reportedly was the first person to introduce Queen Victoria to the taste of that exotic fruit. All of these delights were wrapped in a genuine piece of sari material that Melanie imported from India.

A great deal of fun – and, most importantly, the chocolates were absolutely delicious. And not a one-off, though subsequent inspiration has sometimes come from close to Melanie's Helensburgh home.

"I was walking one day in the rugged woodland around Loch Lomond," she told me, "and I saw wildflowers and fruit growing together: wild brambles – blackberries – growing alongside meadowsweet. That was a combination that I had never tasted, but I put them together with a Madagascan-origin dark chocolate, and it worked so well."

Travelling further afield in the UK and abroad has inspired other collections: from Morocco, a bar made with ras el hanout spice blended with wild Japanese rose petals, foraged around Helensburgh. "I combined those with a robust dark chocolate from São Tomé, providing warmth and a rich cocoa body to the bar."

As well as foraging, Melanie grows many of her ingredients: an ever-changing line-up of herbs and berries ranging from raspberries to white currants.

When it comes to the cocoa: "I have to know where it comes from, how it has been grown, what processes it has gone through, how the plantation is cared for – and whether the farmers and employees are receiving fair pay. It's important for me, and one of the reasons I started to make bean-to-bar chocolate. I like to know exactly what has been put into the final product."

CocoaMo is still a one-woman operation: Melanie still tempers all her chocolate by hand, and packs every box and bar herself. Now that she is supplying a good number of 5-star hotels with 'turn-down' chocolates (those little treats left on your pillow), that can be 1,500 bars for that purpose alone. On the plus side, she is getting fan mail – several emails a month from chefs wanting to come and work with her.

But for now, she has no plans to expand her venture. "I've lost count of the number of people – members of the public, hoteliers and chefs – who have told me with such enthusiasm to 'Stay small, stay unique, don't change what you're doing!' So I won't! It works for me…"

It can be hard work, without a doubt. And in her spare time, Melanie is training hard at taekwondo and often travelling to represent her country in the sport. But whenever her energy flags, she remembers her late mother, the 'Mo' in the company's name.

"My mother and I shared a passion for all things sweet and indulgent, whether in pastry or chocolate form," Melanie recalled. "We'd bake together, and those were the days I enjoyed the most: making recipes that were handed down from her mother. We would make everything from Lancashire hotpot, that aroma of beef and potatoes that's so comforting – and one of my father's favourites – to parkin and treacle toffee."

In particular, Melanie remembers a day in 2008 when her mother came to visit and the two of them spent the day cooking. "She said that she admired how adventurous I was with food, and how confident and relaxed I seemed to be in the kitchen."

Melanie had bought some lovely artisan chocolates to have with coffee, and they prompted a remark that has stuck with her, and to this day provides motivation for her collections:

"Chocolate can evoke happy memories and satisfy our cravings," her mother said. "But when it's done right, it can leave a person never wanting it to end..."

> " Chocolate can evoke happy memories and satisfy our cravings," her mother said. "But when it's done right, it can leave a person never wanting it to end...

That was to be the last time that the two of them cooked together. Melanie's mother passed away from non-Hodgkin lymphoma in 2009, at the age of 53. "My mother never had the opportunity to see this company I created in her name," Melanie said. "But I like to think that she would be my best customer if she was still with us today."

I've no doubt that's true. And I'm sure she'd be darn proud of her daughter as well.

The landscape around Helensburgh that so inspires Melanie Neil is surrounded by water – the great expanse of Loch Lomond behind the town, and vast sea lochs and the sea itself in front.

But my third champion of Scottish chocolate occupies a different landscape altogether, one that is included with pride in the title of his business, because Iain Burnett is the Highland Chocolatier.

I first came across Iain a few years back when I was a judge in a slightly peculiar competition called the Great British Salted Chocolate Challenge, which inspired – if that is the word I am after – some fairly peculiar entries. But the Highland Chocolatier (who travelled down for the final with full chef's gear, which he wore to the ceremony, complete with tall chef's toque) was the clear winner, with a fine double entry: a salted raspberry and peppers truffle, paired with a lime and chilli white chocolate. These were, I wrote in the *Telegraph* at the time, "ultra-professional creations, carried off with finesse, subtlety and Michelin-level delicacy."

As I would subsequently discover, they were also entirely typical of Iain's work. By choice, he is not a bean-to-bar chocolate maker, though his respect for fine single-origin cacao is immense. Instead, he has chosen to become one of the world's finest exponents of that delicious chocolate creation, the truffle.

Many who make these delicate items – essentially chocolate and cream, whipped together and covered with powder, or enrobed in more chocolate – have trained as chef-patissiers. But Iain's background is quite different.

"I was brought up on the West Coast of Scotland," he told me. "My father was a seaman, he trained people to sail, aboard a gaff-rigged ketch. He was a cook – a cook, mind you, not a chef. But he had a thing about always using local ingredients, and I used to help in the kitchen.

"He had a particular style of cooking that I think rubbed off on me, and my mother is a perfectionist – and that rubbed off too. But I didn't train as a chef or patissier – I trained as a product design engineer, and that has been a huge influence in the way that I go about things in the kitchen, and it has certainly come in useful."

Later on in life, Iain trained in all the different styles of chocolate making: "In the Swiss style, the Belgian style, making the whole gamut of chocolates. I found that what I did best was making ganaches, and that is pretty much what I do now."

And so he does, in style. A tall, imposing man with a somewhat serious expression, he has set up an experimental kitchen, chocolate museum and luxurious shop on the outskirts of Pitlochry, a smart little town on the River Tummel, close to beautiful, towering mountains.

There is a healthy clientele locally for his creations, among the residents and the numerous smart hotels, with a healthy throughput of tourists throughout the year drawn by the hiking and the fishing. But it is the raw materials that are the draw for the Highland Chocolatier.

"This is the food basket of Scotland, the Tay Valley," Iain explained. "This is where all the best berries come from, this is where the apiaries are for the best heather honey, the best dairies. Really, everything that a truffle specialist could ever need is here or hereabouts."

The other great bonus of a rural location – and how often have I heard this from chocolate makers? – is the lifestyle. "My staff are here because the lifestyle suits them, and it's important to me – and to what we do – that they stick around," Iain said.

Chefs in training like to do a year or so in one place – a *stage* – before moving on to another to pick up more skills. But Iain's set-up requires a longer-term commitment. "It can take three years to train someone to do what we do," he said. "And a lot of people, particularly young chefs, are looking to do a *stage* here, a *stage* there, one year here, one year there, and that just won't work with what we do. It can be very difficult in this industry to retain staff, but if they like the lifestyle here, and they have the patience…"

Clearly they do. It's an unusual line-up, but notable for dedication and staying-power: "I have an ex-nurse, a former pastry chef – and the lady who used to be the cleaner! They're here because it works for them. They enjoy the detail, I think, and they have to be patient."

That patience is required because the Highland Chocolatier has standards of excellence that would make a multiple-Michelin-starred chef blush, and a curiosity for scientific experiment that would grace a Nobel-winning laboratory.

The scientific angle has its roots in his early training, but the pursuit of excellence can probably be traced to the time that he spent with his wife in Japan before setting out on his truffle career. "We thought of settling there, but for one reason or another we came back to Scotland," he explained. "But I found our time there very special and inspiring. When it comes to true specialist chocolate making, the Japanese set the bar very high – very high indeed. You know, I look at a chocolate there and think: 'This must have taken a week to make. How do you do that?' I love it."

On their return, Iain threw himself into his research. "I was particularly interested in the making of truffles, and all the possibilities of that – how do you make a beautiful truffle without a shell, without any additives? I spent about three years, with backing from my mother, who was very patient about seeing a return on her investment, working on the velvet truffle that I had in mind, making about 150 refinements to the process until I had something that I was happy with."

The next step was to take what he had made to the Gleneagles Hotel, arguably the most prestigious in Scotland. "And they liked it – and that's how it went…"

These days, a lot of Iain's business lies in supplying luxury hotels and restaurants with beautiful truffles. But don't think for a moment that because he has achieved what anyone would regard as success, the experimentation has stopped. The fascination of the process still has him in thrall.

"As you know, Andrew, of all the chocolates that you can make, ganaches are the most awkward. Crystallising a ganache is a real challenge." And the challenge, of course, is what he adores. "It is hugely complex, because you are working with cocoa butter, and then if you introduce dairy butter into that, or cream, the problems become much, much more complicated because of the way these things work together. How to keep the purity? I really enjoy the science behind problems such as that."

Iain is not really into crazy, gimmicky flavours: as he pointed out, he's not going to spend his time introducing a garlic-flavoured patchouli-stick chocolate. What he likes to play with are issues at the most technical level – the micro-level.

"Maybe that's why I've had the same team for five or six years," he said. "There are four of us in the kitchen, and we have a 45-minute meeting every single week to look at slight adjustments and improvements in what we do. There is a *lot* of tweaking and many slight adjustments."

These are not undertaken purely in the pursuit of scientific excellence, but because, like all chocolatiers, Iain is working with ingredients that are themselves subject to change.

"I use a lot of chocolate from São Tomé, and that can change a little over time according to how it was harvested, stored and fermented and so on," he pointed out. But the main changes are in the cream.

> " I have an ex-nurse, a former pastry chef – and the lady who used to be the cleaner! They're here because it works for them. They enjoy the detail, I think, and they have to be patient

THE HIGHLAND
Burnett
CHOCOLATIER
THE HIGHLAND CHOCOLATIER

"Let me tell you about cream. Cream for a truffle chef is *very* important." When the team were looking for the best materials, they held a big blind tasting. At one end of the cream scale they found "pretty unimpressive stuff, supermarket quality, stuff that tasted like sour milk, dreadful". But right at the other extreme was "this wonderful cream, which tasted like Greek yoghurt with honey – sweet and grassy, like that stem of grass that you chewed as a child, just wonderful. And this wonderful cream came from just a couple of valleys away."

> **" Iain has, he shyly admits, made "a few chocolates" for Mark Flanagan, chef to Her Majesty the Queen**

The underlying reason is that a lot of dairy producers blend their product together with cream from other producers – often by the tanker-load. "But this lovely stuff came from a family set-up with a big, healthy herd on good pasture, and they didn't mix what they produced with other farmers' cream – thank goodness.

"So that's what we use. And it's really good. Don't get me wrong though – I don't use local raw materials just because they're local – I use them because they're good. I want to produce the best chocolates that I possibly can, all the time, so I choose what I need to be the best."

But things change. Cream just does – naturally, with the weather, with what the cows are grazing on, and so on. That is as it should be, and it's a wonderful thing – but it is a real challenge for the chocolatier. The São Tomé chocolate changes a little, and then the cream changes, and that gives a kind of seasonality to what Iain and his team are making – but on a micro-level.

Such a dedicated pursuit of excellence has been recognised not only by the best of Scotland's chefs, but also by a notable (part-time) resident. Iain has, he shyly admits, made "a few chocolates" for Mark Flanagan, chef to Her Majesty the Queen.

Happily, the more humble among us can still expect a welcome in the grand style if we pay a state visit to Pitlochry. What Iain calls 'a wee shop' is actually a very smart set-up indeed, an elegant showroom/boutique, and alongside is the

Chocolate Centre, essentially a living museum with sculptures, interactive screens and videos that explain what gourmet artisan chocolates are and how they are made. And not just what Iain and his team get up to, but also something of bean-to-bar and tree-to-bar approaches.

"We've found that when I can take the time to explain to people why and how we do what we do, they just love it," Iain said. "We made the exhibition initially for the chefs who take our chocolates to serve in their restaurants, but the public really go for it as well, old and young – anyone from 10 years old or so onwards and upwards."

Next up is a sampling experience to go with it, an audio-guided tasting process that features a 'flight' of chocolates – just as wine fans can have a wine flight or whisky lovers a whisky flight.

This idea came out of another big part of what Iain does, which is pairing chocolates with drinks. "It's great to pair a ganache of a particular kind with a suitable drink," he explained. "These new flavours just fly out at you. The distilleries love it – we've worked with Glenmorangie, Dalmore, The Macallan – and it is not just great whisky fans. People who are not big whisky drinkers, or even don't drink it at all, find that just nosing a whisky alongside the right chocolate can open up an amazing experience."

For myself, I'm content with the amazing experience of diving into one of Iain's truffles. But I love the way that he is taking the trouble to explain to his audience the whole range of delights that chocolate has to offer.

And I love the way that he and his team understand – just as the chocolate makers do at Chocolarder in Cornwall far to the south, and all the other busy artisans do in between – that if you share your joy in chocolate, and explain a little about what makes it so special, you can only win more converts to the cause.

☐ Chocolate Tree's range of bars is extensive and includes not only the organic line-up and single-origin bean-to-bar creations but also bars flavoured with complementary ingredients, such as pineapple and orange. In a nod to their Scottish roots they do an earth-dark bar flavoured with whisky, and boozy creations closer to the roots of the cacao with pisco and mezcal flavourings.

☐ My favourites among their current bean-to-bar selection are both from Peru – the lovely dark Chililique and the 60% Marañón dark milk, a lovely gentle number redolent of dried summer fruits, which fuelled most of the composition of this chapter.

TASTING NOTES

☐ A unique feature of Chocolate Tree's bars is that they come in twin packs: square-shaped 80g cartons (decorated with Freddy's stylish graphics) that contain two individually wrapped oblong 40g bars. I find that I can usefully distract colleagues by hurling them one bar while I consume the other by myself. Those with more self-restraint can get two days' quality chocolate from each pack – and those packs are keenly priced, at £4.95–£5.95 from the Chocolate Tree website.

☐ Typical of small-scale producers, Melanie Neil is much influenced by the freshest raw materials she can get her hands on, including what she forages from the loch shores and hillsides in her area. The CocoaMo menu changes frequently – of the most recent line-up at the time of writing I can heartily recommend her layered chocolate bonbon made with a base of salted caramel and topped with a kalamansi ganache, all enrobed (I love that word) in a dark single-origin chocolate from Vietnam.

□ The Highland Chocolatier is a world-leading specialist in the area of truffles and you would be bonkers not to try his trademark velvet truffles, which may well change the way you think about luxury chocolates.

□ The levels of commitment and skill that go into making these chocolates are extraordinary. I have tasted many chocolate truffles, some the work of chefs with multiple Michelin stars, but I have never tasted any that combine smooth, delicate texture with deep flavour in the manner of Iain's sublime creations. But don't take my word for it. Head for Pitlochry – and if you can't get up there this weekend, get online at highlandchocolatier.com, where you can order half a dozen truffles for £10.95. Frankly, though, I wouldn't want to order fewer than a dozen, at £19.95. For research and comparative purposes, of course – by now, you will be familiar with my methods…

EPILOGUE

That will have to do, for now. I can't think of a better way of touring Britain than joining the dots between lovely chocolate makers, and I earnestly hope that many people will be inspired to devise their own chocolate-oriented itinerary.

But I have to pause to share out my goodies, and give the car's suspension a rest, and rebalance my diet ever so slightly towards things that aren't chocolate. Not for long, though…

I restricted my visiting list for this book to bean-to-bar makers (with one or two worthy exceptions, notable for other reasons). That was severe, perhaps, but I wanted to capture the spirit of a new direction in ethical, engaged chocolate making that is still on the rise, one in which Britain is leading the way.

In so doing I know I was excluding a great many worthy makers of beautiful chocolates. I'm thinking of places such as Sylvia & Terry's in Dymchurch in Kent – purely for example – a smashing shop where the chocolates include local ingredients, the welcome is warm and everyone concerned has their heart in the right place. There are many other such set-ups, giving a lot of pleasure at the heart of their communities.

So I want to encourage everyone who cares about chocolate to get involved with their local makers and retailers, whether they are purist bean-to-bar pioneers or traditional buy-it-in, melt-it-down, make-funny-shapes-with-it operators.

Shop local! Visit in person, and talk to the people making and selling. Tell them what you love about what they do, and what you'd like them to do in the future.

If your local chocolate-shop-keeper is one of those who still believe that, in chocolate terms, 'Belgian' is synonymous with 'classy', have a quiet word. Tell them, with my blessing, that this truly is no longer the case, and suggest one or two alternative suppliers from closer at hand than Brussels or Ostend.

Go to farmers' markets and food fairs and talk to stallholders who are selling chocolate, especially if they have made it themselves. This is where you will find the adventurous souls who are taking the first steps towards becoming an established independent maker. Help them to make a difference.

Or make a difference yourself. It is easy – as I have found – to get involved with the world of real chocolate. As well as enthusiastic makers, there are tour guides and tasting experts and an Academy full of enthusiasts who are longing to make new converts to a cause that they believe in.

Get along to tastings, have a go at judging, or learn the skills of roasting, tempering and making your own bars, filled chocolates or truffles. You could be a candidate for the second edition…

If you really can't get out and about, get involved online. Many artisan makers have terrific websites, and cocoarunners.com is a brilliant resource for supplies and information.

Above all, put down the tasteless gunk made by faceless multinationals and seek out the good stuff. Support your local makers, who craft chocolate in the right way, with care and respect for those who grow and supply the raw materials, and the energy, skill and patience to make those materials into delicious delights.

The future of good chocolate is in your hands. Don't let it melt away.

ACKNOWLEDGEMENTS

My thanks to all the chocolate makers who welcomed me to their homes, workshops, sheds and factories, and who helped me in so many other ways with advice, hospitality – and chocolate.

As well as those mentioned in the text I would like to thank Sara Jayne Stanes OBE, Silvija Davidson and Marie-Pierre Moine of the Academy of Chocolate; Chantal Coady OBE; Simon Wright; Jennifer Earle of Chocolate Ecstasy Tours; Hazel Lee; Kate Johns; the knowledgeable and kindly Spencer Hyman of Cocoa Runners; Charlotte Borger of Divine; Judith Lewis, who blogs brilliantly at mostlyaboutchocolate.com; Zoe Perrett, aka The Cocoa Nut; Ecuador's finest ambassador, Susana Cardenas; Amelia Rope; and the wonderful Megan Roberts of Hotel Chocolat. Huge thanks to Hugh Bonneville for timely lunches and editorial input.

This book was the brainchild of Donna Wood, who has been a kindly, encouraging and diligent editor throughout; I would also like to acknowledge – and recommend – books by Dom Ramsey (*Chocolate*) and Megan Giller (*Bean to Bar Chocolate: America's Craft Chocolate Revolution*).

Thanks to my colleagues at the *Telegraph*, who have stoically assisted with many hours' tasting down the years, and helped in many other ways: Paul Davies, Keith Miller, Anna Murfet, Olivia Walmsley, Boudicca Fox-Leonard, Amy Bryant, Tom Ough, Pip Sloan, Anna Tyzack, Kylie Sanderson and Olivia Parker have all 'done their bit'.

At home, Ingrid Bleichroeder and our daughters Lucy and Emily (abetted by Sammy the cockapoo) have tolerated the grumpy author with remarkable grace, as have my brother James and sister- and brother-in-law Kathryn and Stuart Sanders.

Errors that remain are mine alone; it has been a very enjoyable book to write.

PICTURE CREDITS